Deploying Enterprise Systems

This book focuses on topics that business managers and project teams in global enterprises need to understand and follow to successfully build and deploy an Enterprise System (ES) for their organization. It explains why this type of software product will appeal to global organizations with the promise to replace their older individual systems with a single integrated ES. An ES allows companies to integrate their unique operations with a single system of many integrated modules that are designed to provide prebuilt and tested applications; new concepts, steps, and methods that an organization should follow to successfully create and deploy an ES and the reasons that ES projects fail and the practices to manage these risks. In addition, the book describes a new implementation model and methods to ensure success to deploy an ES across a firm with several divisions, international operations, product lines, or infrastructure. Essentially, this book:

- Describes, in nontechnical terms, what business functions this new software product will improve
- Shows how an enterprise should use this software product to accomplish their goals to install and use this new technology to upgrade their older systems
- Explains what an organization's management and project teams should avoid during selecting, planning, and implementing their ES to avoid common mistakes
- Describes the skills and experience the project manager must have to lead the project team(s) to implement this advanced system.

Deploying Enterprise Systems

How to Select, Configure, Build, Deploy, and Maintain a Successful ES in Your Organization

David Mattson

Routledge
Taylor & Francis Group

A PRODUCTIVITY PRESS BOOK

First published 2024
by Routledge
605 Third Avenue, New York, NY 10158

and by Routledge
4 Park Square, Milton Park, Abingdon, Oxon, OX14 4RN

Routledge is an imprint of the Taylor & Francis Group, an informa business

ISBN: 978-1-032-46421-3 (hbk)
ISBN: 978-1-032-46420-6 (pbk)
ISBN: 978-1-003-38161-7 (ebk)

DOI: 10.4324/9781003381617

Typeset in Garamond
by Newgen Publishing UK

This book is dedicated to Tricia for her
love and encouragement

Contents

About the Author

David Mattson is a graduate of the University of Pennsylvania with an undergraduate BS in Engineering and a MBA from Wharton School. He has 30 years' experience deploying information systems for large global enterprises, medium and startup firms, hospitals, universities, and nonprofits.

His qualification for this subject includes leading Enterprise Systems (ES) projects for J&J, Federal Express, Gillette, and several startup firms. He has also directed multiple projects to replace an organization's ERP system with a new ES of integrated applications. During his career, he has directed IT projects and programs for

- Client projects for two major consulting firms (BearingPoint and CSC)
- ES projects with staffs of 5–20 and budgets $1M–$20M
- ES for human resources, finance, purchasing, supply chain, manufacturing, sales, marketing, and R&D

He resides in New York City.

Chapter 1

The Challenge to Deploy Enterprise Systems

CHALLENGES DEPLOYING ENTERPRISE SYSTEMS

- Lack of business leader's commitment and continuous support
- Failure to set realistic goals and expectations
- Choosing ES product that requires more than 10% customization

1.1   Introduction

Enterprise systems (ES) are a new type of commercially available software products that help an enterprise integrate their systems and operations, streamline business processes, manage data, and track results. Over the past 15 years, Enterprise Systems with prebuilt applications have evolved to become a new software technology that allows an organization to replace stand-alone systems with a suite of prebuilt, tested, and supported applications for business, non profit, and government enterprises without needing an internal software team to develop and maintain a custom-built system. When used correctly, ES allow enterprises to replace individual outdated (legacy) systems across the enterprise to better realize their strategic goals and expand their mission. They are designed to support enterprise-wide operations, rather than separate operations or processes. A wide

DOI: 10.4324/9781003381617-1

variety of ES solutions have been developed to enable businesses, nonprofits and government organizations become more competitive and fulfill their mission by integrating their business functions to speed up of their goods and services. Enterprise Systems have replaced software packages called Enterprise Resource Planning (ERP) which have been available since the 1990s. These packages only integrated one or two business operations for a business such as finance and human resource operations. However, many of today's ERP products provide a suite of applications that qualify as Enterprise Systems. To achieve the potential benefits of deploying their ES, each organization must meet several challenges. These challenges include:

- Complexity. ES are complex software products. Implementing an integrated system successfully requires a large investment of money, time, technical and business expertise, and continuous attention of management.
- Impact. ES will have an impact on the enterprise's organization, culture, and business processes.
- Competitive Advantage. ES imposes generic (common) processes across all business units and geography when unique customized are required for a competitive advantage.
- Fully Qualified Project Manager. A highly qualified project manager, with both business and technology skills, must be assigned to lead the implementation of an ES.
- Leadership. Management and participants in the project must clearly understand the unique implementation process for an ES.
- Correct Choice. Choosing the wrong ES which results in a mismatch between the organization's goals or implementing this new technology incorrectly can severely disrupt operations, reduce employee productivity, and waste resources.

1.2 Ten Reasons Enterprise Systems Projects Fail[1]

Industry studies have identified ten reasons that ES implementations fail to meet their original planned goals, benefits, and critical timeline. These reasons include:

- Failure of organization to embrace change
- Lack of commitment from senior management and key stakeholders

- Assigning project manager who lacks needed skills, experience, and accountability to make timely decisions
- Not aligning ES requirements with organization's Long Range goals
- Insufficient Funding. Not using a buffer for costs and schedule over runs
- Lack of investment in change management
- Insufficient testing
- Failure to adequately train users of the new system
- Poor Software Fit. Selecting an ES product that requires more than 10% customization
- Insufficient team resources and skills

1.3   Benefits and Risks to Deploy an Enterprise System

ES provide both significant benefits but also costly unanticipated risks for any organization adopting this integrated system. Table 1.1 summarizes many of these benefit and risks. Later chapters offer methods and practices to achieve these benefits and reduce many of the risks.

Table 1.1   Benefits and Risks of Enterprise Systems

Business Benefits	Risks
Replace different systems across the enterprise with applications from a single vendor's Common System software.	Imposing generic processes across all business units when some customized functions allow features that help maintain a competitive advantage.
Sharing information across functional departments will break up silos of information resulting in sharing data and more cooperation to solve problems.	Departments may make a mistake in sharing proprietary data within the organization.
Centralize data across functional departments.	System security will be more complex. An ES requires revised and updated security protocols for its modular systems, data, and computer networks. The new ES system may require programmed interfaces with other systems and data bases, be compatible with enterprise communications network, add require new software and hardware to the current security requirements.

(Continued)

Table 1.1 **(Continued)**

Business Benefits	Risks
Offer industry best practices. The software functions are designed to reflect the vendor's selection of the best practices for business processes.	The organization must be careful not to adopt new practices which reduce a competitive advantage.
ES product updates add new functions and technology vendor invests in product research and new technology to extend product for customers.	An ES support team may have difficulty keeping up with each new ES release across the enterprise. The internal oversite group must decide whether to add new functions and technology and schedule to update new version across the enterprise.
Earlier completion and launch of an integrated system. The pre built solution allows the enterprise to complete and deploy a new system faster and with fewer software defects (bugs).	ES products vary in how conveniently the customer can modify these practices.
Early adopter of ES product's new features and technology. A firm may choose to be one of the first customers to implement an early or new version of an ES product that includes new modules or software technology (smartphones).	An early adopter of software product and technology adds significant risk for any enterprise. Like all major changes for an enterprise, deploying a complex new system may cause unexpected disruptions to normal operations, e.g., year-end operations. In many functional areas, employees will have to use both their current system to conduct business and invest additional effort for training and parallel operation of the new ES.
	Other Risks
	■ An ES product and vendor may lock an organization into risks including the high cost of switching to another product in the future. ■ The vendor may be acquired by a larger ES vendor that freezes upgrades for your installed version.

1.4 Translate Organization's Long-Range Goals to Enterprise Systems Requirements

Small organizations or start up firms do not need a Long Range Plan to define the key requirements for an ES. Often the firm wants to automate an essential core function like accounting to replace the burden for the staff to prepare many spreadsheets.

Large and medium-size companies, nonprofits, and government organizations deploy ES to help achieve their long-range plans and missions. Their plans are based on different initiatives such as

- an in-depth review of the organization's current operating plan
- recommendations of a task force or commission

Whatever the basis for their plan, the ES project team must first identify the goals to accomplish the plan's vision; then map each goal to operational objectives the firm wants to achieve in the next 2–3 years. The third task is the ES project team to define requirements (first high level then detailed) for the ES solution. These requirements are the basis to select, configure, and deploy the new system within the enterprise.

Before starting to select the ES solution the firm's Selection Team (Program Sponsor, Steering Committee, and representatives for each stakeholders) should map the firm's strategic goals to operational objectives and macro requirements for the ES. This model will help ensure the enterprise's long-range goals are linked to the requirements for the ES solution:

- Each goal of the LR Plan should define one or more operational objectives in the firm's operating pan for the next 1–3 years.
- The final link requires the ES project team to define one or more system requirements for the ES.

Figure 1.1 shows this model to link the firm's strategic plan and goals to the requirements for the ES.

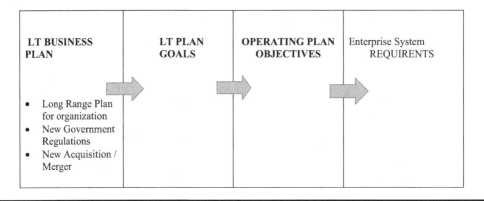

Figure 1.1   Linking organization's strategic plan to ES requirements.

1.5   The Audience for This Book

The audience for this book are include the following members of the organization who are important to the success of an ES endeavor:

- Executives who will back the multiyear endeavor.
- Strategic planning staff will help match the long-range goals and direction to the key functions of the ES.
- Project sponsor and project Steering Committee members, who will lead the program to ensure its success.
- Program/project managers, who will manage the implement of the enterprise system.
- ES implementation team members who must understand the technology and build the new systems.
- Stakeholders, who will need to understand the functions and features of these new systems and how they will impact and change their operations.
- Consultants and ES vendor personnel who support the enterprise's implementation effort, and need to understand the organization's goals and challenges driving the ES program that will help deliver success.

Executives of these organizations have questions they want answered before giving their approval and strong backing to launch an ES program:

- Does this technology support our strategic plan to expand our organization, mission, customer base, or other goals?

- How closely will the features, functions, and technology of these software packages help achieve our key goals, objectives, and initiatives for the next 2–3 years it may take to complete this program?
- What is the investment (operating and capital) that is required to implement this technology and how will this impact our financial plan and operating budget this year and for the next 2–3 years?
- How should this significant investment be allocated/charged to our divisions or operating units? Should this investment be funded from each unit's budget (which impacts net operating profit) or by a corporate expense account that is charged back to operating units?
- Who should lead this program (the Sponsor) and which senior managers should be on the Steering Committee? How will we keep the strategic planning group together to lead the multiyear program to roll out the ES system?
- Should we hire an experienced consulting firm like Accenture or IBM to help us assess our requirements and select an ES package for us, or rely on an internal team?

The Sponsor and Steering Committee members have most of the same questions as the senior executives. They have their own questions about leading this critically important enterprise program/project:

- What do we need to know about this ES technology to understand the complexity, rewards, and risks for this program/project?
- Who are the groups and individuals who have a stake in the successful outcome of this ES project? Who will support the project and who has issues about this endeavor?
- What is the strategy to organize this massive endeavor?
- Should we begin by implementing the functions before a rollout for other parts of our operation?
- Should we install the entire ES in a single division first then deploy before beginning to implement for the ES applications in other division?

The operating level managers have most of the same questions as the organization's senior executives:

- How will this new ES support our current tactical plans and annual objectives? *What's in it for me (WIIFM)?*

- How will the commercial ES product be selected? Can someone in my group help evaluate and select it?
- How closely will the features and functions of this new software help improve operations and provide additional information not provided by our current legacy systems?
- Who can I spare to join the project team to make sure we get the new features and valuable information from the ES? What percentage of our representative's time can we spare to participate – 20%, more?
- How disruptive will this new system be to my staff? What training will be needed?

The IT leadership of the organization (CIO and Senior IT Directors of operating units) have questions they want answered about the new ES and technology they will have responsibility to successfully deliver:

- Should we use internal or external personnel for this project or programs? Options – in-house IT staff, outside consulting firm (onsite, offsite, offshore), software vendor?
- What's best alternative to provide computing and network support to run the ES? Options – build out our current IT infrastructure, use a remote data center or cloud computing vendor, or rely on the vendor to operate the ES for us?
- Should we accept the vendor's software standards used to create and maintain the ES product including databases, programming language, open-source code, etc.?
- What should be the team organization structure for this initiative – program office, project team?
- Who should be assigned to lead the implementation? Which key management and technology skills should they have?
- Which stakeholders may not support their organization adopting the new ES if it will replace their current systems, procedures, or staff? How should we help them get onboard?

1.6 Organization of This Book

Each chapter helps explain unique challenges to adopt an ES and provides commonsense methods and tools to help meet these challenges.

Chapter 1: The Challenge to Deploy Enterprise Systems

Describes what ES are and why this new software technology is important to the success of an enterprise.

Chapter 2: Organize and Manage Enterprise System Projects

Describes the unique ES implementation project cycle method. Covers the role, responsibility, and contribution for each key member of the project organization during the ES implementation. Emphasizes the business and technical skills that Project Managers need to successfully manage an ES project.

Chapter 3: Choose Software

Describes the steps to search for information about competitive products and complete the selection of an ES.

Chapter 4: Plan ES Project

Lists the steps the ES project team should complete to successfully launch and complete the implementation of an ES. The emphasis is on the steps to plan the full implementation of this software.

Chapter 5: Design Enterprise System

Describes methods to define the requirements for the design of the ES solution for your enterprise. It includes the description of a novel method (Deep Dive) to match the organization's detailed requirements to the ES functions and features.

Chapter 6: Build and Test Enterprise System

Describes the unique methods required to build and test an ES. This includes building and testing four components:

- Configure functions
- Customized features
- Data migration
- Interfaces to other systems

Chapter 7: Deploy the Enterprise System

Covers the steps to deploy the new ES system after completing the testing and plans to deploy the new system and set up a Help Desk and operations team to support updates to the new system.

Chapter 8: Close Enterprise Project Cycle

Describes the activities to wrap up the current project cycle and begin planning the next project cycle.

1.7   Summary

ES allow organizations to implement a full suite of software applications from the same vendor with less risks and business interruption. This book pulls together practical advice, methods, and helpful tools to manage projects for business, nonprofit, and government organizations.

Note

1 After *top 10 reasons for implementation failure (and how to avoid it)*, ERP Focus, July 22, 2022.

Chapter 2

Organize and Manage ES Projects

CHALLENGES DEPLOYING ES

- Lack of commitment by senior management and key stakeholders
- Assigning project manager who lacks needed skills and experience
- Using current standard implementation process and not project cycle process or ES projects

---

This chapter describe methods, good practices, and tools to organize and manage small, medium, or large projects to deploy complex enterprise software. It describes the management skills a Project Manager (PM) should use to minimize common problems and to successfully complete the ES project.

A project is a one-time initiative that organizations carry out to create an unique product, service, or result. Projects have defined start and finish dates, achieve a desired objective, and delivere a required result. However, a project to create an ES, that will link most operations and is deployed to all parts of an enterprise, is an endeavor to deploy an application that may take years to complete.

DOI: 10.4324/9781003381617-2

1 ORGANIZE THE ES PROJECT

The ES PM is responsible for organizing the project which includes

- Define the ES project life cycle
- Establish roles and responsibilities for primary participants
- Prepare the Project Organization Chart

2.1 Enterprise Systems Project Cycle

Most software development projects follow a standard process called the Software Development Life Cycle (SDLC). The SDLC framework organizes a project into discrete phases which are initiate, plan, design, build, test, deploy, support, and close.

For ES projects, the process differs from the SDLC model and follows a different sequence of steps, which allow multiple applications to deploy as separate project cycles. Figure 2.1 shows a Project Management Framework for ES projects.

2.2 Define Roles and Responsibilities

The roles and responsibilities (R&R) for key participants in an ES project are the same as most software implementation projects. There are additional responsibilities for some team members for selecting and implementing this software technology.

The key R&R for an ES endeavor are:

- Executive sponsor
- Project sponsor
- Project Steering Committee
- PM
- Project stakeholders
- ES users
- Project teams
- ES vendor

Organize Project	Choose ES	Plan ES Project	Define ES	Build & Test ES	Deploy & Maintain ES	Complete ES Project Cycle & Plan Next Cycle
Define Roles Responsibilities	Project Charter	Project Plan Documents	Deep Dive Review	ES Configure	Deploy Plan Training Plan	Close Current Project Cycle
Define Project Organization	Select ES Solution	Project Scope	Requirement Spec	ES Customize	System Launch	– Archive Docs – Close accounts Contracts
Assign Exec & Project Sponsors		Project Sched		Data Migration	Support Plan	– Final Reports
Chose / Hire Project Mgr.		Requirement Trace Matrix		Test Plan	Help Desk	
		Project Kickoff		Test Results	S/W Maintenance Procedure	Plan Next Project Cycle
		Project Staffing				

Figure 2.1 ES project cycle.

Executive Sponsor

The executive sponsor is a member of senior management for the enterprise. They include the CEO, CFO, CIO, and head of business or organization units. Their *role* is to initiate, champion, and provide senior management backing for the ES project. Their *responsibility* is to approve the business case for the project and confirm that the selection for the ES will support the organization's strategic plans, approve the funding for the project, and back this initiative within the enterprise.

Project Sponsor

The project sponsor's *role* is to lead the project and make sure it meets the objectives set by senior management and the Steering Committee. The sponsor also champions the project team's effort and communicates progress to the Steering Committee and senior management. Their *responsibility* is to help the PM obtain funding and resources and to resolve problems, conflicts, and organizational issues.

ES projects create additional challenges for the project sponsor including helping to resolve issues or problems that come up with

- individuals or departments in the enterprise about the impact of the new system on their operations
- ES vendor or implementation consultants

Project Steering Committee

The Steering Committee includes the project sponsor and the managers of departments and business units who have a stake in the outcome of the project. Their *role* is to monitor the progress of the project and ensure that the organization's goals are met. The committee's *responsibility* is to approve the project charter, project timeline, project budget, and change requests (CRs).

The selection and implementation of an ES requires added responsibilities for the Steering Committee including:

- Approve the selection of an ES for the organization based on findings of the selection team.
- Decide the priority and choices for custom changes to the ES system.

Project Manager

The Project Manager's (PM) *role* is to coordinate the tasks and interaction of various parties to accomplish the project's objectives in a way that reduces the risk of delays or overall failure, maximizes benefits, and minimizes costs. The PM is *responsible* to create and maintain a plan to accomplish the goals of the project, manage the resources assigned to the project, and meet the agreed-upon scope, budget, quality, and schedule.

The Project Manager has key responsibilities for monitoring and controlling an ES project including:

- Define and communicate project objectives that are clear and attainable
- Acquire and manage project resources needed to accomplish project objectives including skilled work team, workspace, materials, required information, contract agreements, and technology
- Create and maintain the Project Plan/Schedule for the entire project including in-house teams, third-party contractors, and the ES vendor
- Coordinate the project activities with team leads (business, internal teams and vendors, IT QA, and others) including project schedules, meetings, issue management, etc.
- Meet regularly with the project teams to monitor their progress on scheduled tasks as well as issues and risks that could delay the project
- Manage problems that stakeholders or the ES vendor have in meeting their commitments to provide resources, approve deliverables, and other support
- Review and approve project deliverables for accuracy, completeness, and compliance with SOPs
- Help remove roadblocks for team including issues (technical, business, and organizational), needed resources, or financial constraints
- Report project status (schedule, timeline, results, issues, and costs) to the project team, sponsor, and, Steering Committee.

ES projects create additional challenges including:

- managing multiple teams including outside consultants, vendor resources, and offshore (OS) teams
- Managing the relationship with the ES vendor which may have different goals for meeting the agreed Statement of Work (SOW) (e.g., shift senior team members to another client's project)

ES Users

- End users are individuals in the enterprise whose *role* is to participate during the project to help implement and deploy the ES. They have the *responsibility* to help define the requirements, perform user acceptance testing, resolve issues, and help deploy the new system. They include members of the enterprise who will use the system to accomplish their work.

ES Stakeholders

Project stakeholders are individuals in the enterprise whose *role* is to support the project and help it achieve success. They have the *responsibility* to stay informed about the goals and expected results for the project and to raise issues about the impact of the new system on their group.

ES Users

ES users are members of the enterprise who are in a department that will use the system to accomplish their work. Their *role* during the project is to help the project teams implement and deploy the ES. They have the *responsibility* to help define the requirements, perform user acceptance testing, resolve business and procedural issues, and deploy the new system.

Project Teams

Project teams have the *role* to complete the tasks needed to achieve the results wanted for the project. The teams include internal and external participants. Their *responsibilities* include planning, designing, creating, testing, and deploying the ES process or system needed for the project's success. Large ES projects usually require mutable project teams.

ES Vendor

The ES vendor's *role* is to help their customer (your company) get the full benefit from implementing their ES. Their *responsibility* is to assign highly qualified and experienced employees on your implementation project and to provide access to their product team to help resolve technical issues that come up during implementation and deployment of the ES.

2.3 Create Roles and Responsivity Chart

The organization of the project should include the definition of roles and responsibility for key project team positions. These R&Rs are confirmed and documented and shown in a RACI Chart. It is a useful way to show the responsibility for individuals to complete key tasks and deliverables for the project.

The R&R Matrix lists each type of resource (title/person) that has specific deliverables (Roles) in a matrix format. Each box of the matrix shows the type of action each person (Role) is assigned to complete a deliverable. RACI Charts show the four key responsibilities for each delivered result:

- ■ R – Responsible for doing the tasks to complete the deliverable
- ■ A – Approval for the result achieved
- ■ C – Consulted during the tasks to complete the assignment
- ■ I – Informed of progress during and at the end of assignment

Together, these charts show how the project team is organized. Table 2.1 shows part of a typical RACI Chart for an ES project.

2.4 Define Project Organization Chart

The Project Organization Chart describes how the project teams and individuals from functional groups in the enterprise and outside are organized. This includes showing both direct (solid line) reporting and indirect (dotted line) reporting. Figure 2.2 is an example of organization of the project participants. Specific parts of this organization will actively work together during each phase of the ES project.

Table 2.1 RACI Chart

Project Deliverable	Project Manager	Sponsor	Steering Committee	Project Teams	ES Users	Stake Holders	ES Vendor
Charter	R	A	A				
Scope	R	A	A		R		
Project Schedule	R	A	I	C	I		C
Project Plan	R	I		I			I
ES design	A			R	I	I	I
ES Build and Test	A			R	R		
ES Deployment	A		R	R	R	I	I
System support/Maintenance	I		I	R			C
Close project cycle and plan next cycle	R	IA		R	C		C

Note: A – Approve; C – Contribute; I – Informed; R – Responsible.

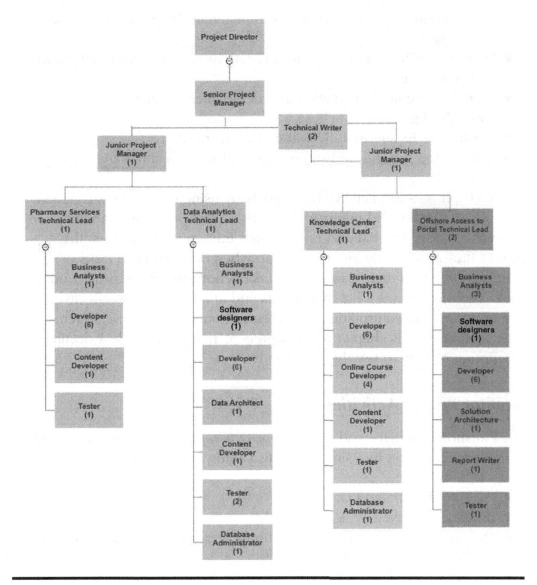

Figure 2.2 Sample ES project organization chart.

II MANAGE THE ES PROJECT

2.5 Monitor and Control Project Tasks

The goal of the monitor and control (M&C) process is to manage the activities of the project team, ES vendor, end users, and other stakeholders so the PM can keep the project on track and deliver the new system successfully. The M&C goals are

- Track progress and correct issues to maintain the project schedule and budget
- Deliver the ES with the approved functions and features (configured and customized)
- Complete the implementation and deployment on time and within budget
- Deploy the ES successfully within the organization
- Achieve the benefits and strategic goals for this technology

The M&C process can achieve these goals by using effective management methods to identify and mitigate issues, risks, and problems, and take corrective action. The PM and project team track progress against the current Project Schedule and take action when deadlines slip tasks or require more effort than planned and take actions to get the project on track. The following is a list of methods and analyses that are effective in monitoring and controlling the implementation of enterprise systems. Later sections of this chapter and Chapters 3, 4, and 5 provide a detailed description of how to use these methods.

Monitor Project Activities

The PM should monitor and track the progress, cost, and results achieved during the ES project by using any of the following documents:

- Project Schedule and Gantt chart
- Baseline approved Project Schedule
- Measures of task completeness – hours and % completed and estimated hours remaining to complete
- Budget vs actual worksheet
- Milestones/deliverables list
- Weekly team status meetings

There are other methods to track the work effort and performance of an ES project; but these are more complex and do not add more information to take corrective action:

- PERT/CPM diagrams
- Earned value analysis

Correct Issues, Problems, and Risks

The methods to identify issues, problems, and risks that will occur during the ES project include:

- Baseline project plan
- Issues and problems log
- Risk register
- Weekly team status meetings

Take Corrective Action

The methods to take corrective action to keep the project on track include:

- Progress status meeting and list of follow-up actions
- Daily five-minute team meeting
- The Friday Rule
- Change request

Report Progress

The methods to report the progress of the project to the Steering Committee and stakeholders include

- Project status/progress reports
- Stop lights chart to show status of critical tasks for project

2.6   Project Management Skills

PMs, who lead complex enterprise system projects, will need more than textbook knowledge of project management principles (Table 2.2).

They will need to use (acquire) two kinds of management skills to successfully lead ES projects:

- Business management skills – Practical methods and skills to manage project, administrative, personnel, other resources and activities

Table 2.2 Project Management Skills

Project Management Skills	*Methods/Tools*
Organize projects	PMBOC standards
	Project scope
	Project plan documents
	Project org chart
	Roles and responsibilities chart
	RACI chart
Manage project teams	Project management plan
	Team contact list
	Team calendar
Manage problems/issues/risks	Problem/issue/risk logs solve problems
Prepare and manage project schedule	PIMBOK Manual (Project Institute Management Body of Knowledge for Project Management)
Manage project changes	Project change procedure
	Project change log
	Project change request (CR)
Manage project documents	Document repository
	Document management software
Manage project communications Manage stakeholder expectations	Project Management Plan (PMP)
	Project team contact list
	Presentations software
	Stakeholder list
Manage budget	Finance requirements
Manage quality	Company SOPs
	Quality audit
Manage procurement	Procurement – contracts/SOWs
	Non-disclosure agreement (NDA)
	Request for proposal (RFP)
	Bidders conference
	Proposal evaluation sheet

needed/required to carry out the ES project. These include planning, organizing, staffing, controlling, and reporting.

■ Project management skills – Skills, methods, practices required to plan, monitor, control, and report project activities including the ES selection, plan, define, build, deploy, and complete phases.

> **TIP** The Project Management Institute publishes The PMBOK Guide which provides a full explanation of the standard practices and methods to M&C a project (Monitoring and Controlling Process Groups) to track, control, and report the progress of a project.

There are many publications written for PMs that explain the process to manage software development projects. Most of these books describe the *technical* steps (procedures) to perform during a project to deliver the software programs, deliverables, documentations, and reports; but don't describe the *business skills and practices* needed to successfully work with stakeholders, vendors, and consultants. For example, software project management texts may describe multiple methods to estimate the effort and time to complete tasks in a Project Schedule, but not how to guide team members who cannot estimate their effort.

2.7 Business Management Skills

All managers, including PMs, must develop and use six core management skills to successfully manage their responsibilities (Table 2.3):

■ Manage your own responsibilities
■ Delegate assignments
■ Manage conflict
■ Manage meetings
■ Navigate corporate culture and politics
■ Follow business etiquette

Table 2.3 Business Management Skills

Business Management Skills	Methods/Tools
Manage your responsibilities	Review job description
	Review responsibilities with your manager
	Confirm responsibilities and annual goals with manager
Delegate assignments	5-step method for delegation
Manage conflict	Negotiation skills/navigate organization's culture and politics
Manage meetings	Presentations software
Navigate enterprise culture and politics	Discussions with peers
Follow business etiquette	Confirm with peers

Manage Your Own Responsibilities

All managers must work cooperatively with others in an organization to meet their responsibilities. These are more personal traits than skills but are the basis to use other skills. These personal traits include:

- Be truthful
- Keep your promises
- Manage your work calendar
- Navigate enterprise culture and politics
- Follow business etiquette

Here are pointers to help managers be successful manage their responsibilities:

- Be truthful. Above all, a manager must tell the truth about small and large events to maintain their credibility.
- Keep your promises. Every manager has assignments that have a specific date to be completed. It is especially important that a PM meet promised due dates for scheduled milestones, decisions, and answers to time critical problems. A manager will lose credibility if they continuously miss promised deadlines for their personal tasks or their team.

- Meet promises. Team members want to depend on your promises to help them manage their tasks
  - technical – get ES vendor to have product engineer help with custom code procedure
  - organizational – get IT Help Desk to provide network printer near team offices

DON'T MISS A DEADLINE TWICE

A manager will have deadlines for the project team to meet project schedule milestones.

- If the PM judges, the teams will not complete a deliverable or milestone by a promised date; then he/she should inform the group, expecting the completed work, well before the deadline. Decide the remaining effort to finish the assignment before you promise a new time.
- As soon as you know your team may or will miss your deadline, inform the people, impacted by the delay, that the team will miss the planned deadline.
- Explain how you can arrange your work or other commitments to finish on time. Ask for their agreement if you want to make this assignment a higher priority than other current priorities.
- Think through your options to complete this task. Estimate the remaining time you or your team needs to complete the task/deliverable. Double check your estimate. Add additional time for contingencies. You can put more time into the assignment by temporarily halting another lower priority task, not attending a training session, etc. You may want to work added hours each day to make up the time you need.
- Commit to make this revised date.

It's crucially important that you do not miss the new promised date. If you do, you damage your credibility.

Delegate Assignments

A successful PM must effectively delegate project tasks (planned and unplanned) to team members.

Many managers mishandle delegation because they do not have enough confidence in their team members or because they do not know or follow the basic principles of delegation. When a manager delegates an assignment incorrectly, the person assigned the task may not receive the essential information to correctly complete the assigned work.

The key to successful delegation is to identify the individual(s) who can conduct the task. Then describe the tasks to be completed including what needs to be done, when the results are needed, and when to keep you informed of their progress. Then as the delegated work is performed, you should provide support to help them complete the task.

Once the task is complete, you will get an opportunity to evaluate their performance and provide constructive feedback.

To effectively delegate an assignment, you should follow these five steps.

- *Describe the task.* Describe exactly *what* you want to be done, *when* you need it completed, and *what* result is expected. Explain why the task needs to be done – describe *why* it contributes to the goals of the project, and why this needs attention now.
- *Provide support.* Determine the resources needed to complete the task and help obtain them. This might be allocation of team members to the task, OK for overtime expense, etc.
- *Give authority.* Give authority necessary for the person to complete the task so they can proceed without having to get your OK for every step for their effort (e.g., to schedule meetings and request help of teammates).
- *Confirm agreement.* Get commitment that the person understands the assignment and accepts responsibility to complete the required effort.
- *Agree when to check progress.* Set time to get updates on progress in completing the delegated task. This could be done at a regular team status meeting or one-on-one meeting. Let the subordinate have input to the timing for progress meetings.

The last two steps are most important. You want to obtain a team member's commitment to complete their assignment, review it with you, and make final changes before they leave for an annual or year-end vacation.

Manage Conflict

A PM must develop the skill to recognize and manage disagreements or conflicts among team members or with stakeholders. During an ES program with multiple teams and individuals in separate segments of the organization, there will be competition for IT resources and competing priorities. Resolving disagreements quickly will help achieve the project's goals and desired outcomes. Try to understand, not only what the other person's opinion about the dispute is but also why both of you cannot reach an agreement.

Here are proven ways to resolve disagreements/conflict that come up during ES projects:

- Seek to understand each side of the issue or disagreement. Then try to find some ways that both of you can agree to try to settle this agreement. If you cannot, then try to find another way to resolve this:
  - Create a CR. The sponsor or a stakeholder wants the team to take on additional requirements or software features which could significantly add to the timeline or approved budget for the project. Or the vendor wants to charge for work that is included in their fixed price SOW agreement. You can resolve many types of disagreements by creating a CR to get an approval for the request or to drop it.
  - Ask others higher up in organization to decide, i.e., agree to disagree. If you cannot resolve the disagreement, document your separate/individual positions and take this to the project sponsors or higher level to help resolve the issue.
- If a conflict becomes personal or heated, first try to settle between you and the other person without involving others. Conflicts can occur with another person for many reasons:
  - Their behavior disrupts the smooth functioning of the project or
  - They challenge your authority as PM to set goals, assign tasks, or deadlines.
- Protect yourself from being misunderstood when there is conflict:
  - Try to resolve misunderstanding by sending a summary of your position and how you both can resolve the conflict.

– Create notes of meetings and phone calls. Summarize your side of the issue or argument and the other person's position. Record if the other person makes a statement you disagree with. Include summaries of discussions or prior emails.

– Create a contemporaneous summary of a discussion about an issue. Send an email to yourself, which will be date stamped, with a copy of your notes.

▪ Keep these types of records during your project, you have the information that you need to provide to your supervisor, project sponsor, or even HR if the dispute cannot be settled.

▪ Backup team members when they have complaints about their work.

Manage Meetings

A PM must coordinate the efforts of a diverse project team (system users, vendors, IT technical staff, and outside consultants) that may be dispersed at several geographic sites. Meetings are an important way to allow a group to collaborate on defining product requirements, review progress, solve difficult issues, and review project work products.

Here is a basic approach to manage project meetings effectively.

▪ *Schedule the meeting to give attendees time to fit it into their calendar.* Check the firm's online calendar or contact individuals to know which dates and times all or most can attend. Send invitations to other individuals who should be informed, but you don't need to attend.

▪ *Prepare for the meeting* to get the outcome you want. State the purpose of the meeting in the announcement (e.g., review project status; review issue and get decision on how to resolve it). Prepare the meeting agenda to cover the topics needed to reach the desired outcome of the meeting and assign yourself or team members to present each topic. Also, you may want to preview your presentation with the project sponsor or other key stakeholder and get their feedback and support for the results you want from the meeting.

▪ *Start the meeting on time and take notes.* Many meetings start late because the meeting leader has difficulty with the mechanics to start a conference call, presentation, or start a video meeting. The PM can avoid this by practicing ahead of time know how to operate the technology, arriving early to check that the equipment needed is there (computer and projector, speakerphone, whiteboard, and markers/eraser), and set up the desktop computer, projector and projection screen, and start a conference call.

- *After the meeting issue minutes.* Assign someone to take minutes during the meeting, including topics discussed, decisions made, and follow-up actions. Send summary minutes to all who were invited to the meeting – even if they did not attend. These minutes should summarize the key points of the meeting along with a copy of the presentation or handouts.

Navigate Enterprise Culture and Politics

The *Merriam-Webster Dictionary* defines Organizational Culture as "the norms, rituals and expected behavior for individuals" who work together in an organization. If they are to be successful, every manager should be aware and adhere to their organization's culture. Managers and employees throughout the organization want to work with a PM who consistently follows corporate norms such as scheduling meetings or celebrating a team's success. For example, your organization's culture may expect you to return phone calls and emails from coworkers by the end of a business day:

- If you are away from your desk for a day or an offsite meeting, consider turning on a message that you are out of touch for communications.
- Reply to calls and requests by the end of normal business day or as soon as you can after the end of the day.
- Make it a priority to respond to requests to confirm a time for a meeting or provide information that is urgently needed.

EXAMPLE

Follow Corporate Culture

About a month after joining an international manufacturing firm, a plant manager called me about 2 pm to arrange a meeting and left a voice mail to call him. This manager was the sponsor for a project I was leading. I was away from my desk attending meetings all afternoon. I returned to my office about 6 pm and checked for my messages. Since it was after normal working hours, I did not call back, text him, or send an email to let him know I had received his voice mail and would call him "first thing" in the morning. The next morning when I got to my office and opened my email, I saw an email he had sent about an hour before, that said in effect that I should have responded to his call by end of the day (EOD) or sent an email that evening so we could update our calendars for appointments. I called him immediately, apologized. His comment revealed two rules for this company's corporate culture:

- colleagues expect a response by the end of the day, when they call, stop by your office, or send an email, even if it is just to acknowledge that it was received.
- managers expect prompt RSVPs throughout the workday for their meeting requests.

Follow Business Etiquette

Regardless of your organization's unique culture, a manager should follow commonsense business etiquette in working with others. Basically, this means that managers (and all of us) should treat other people with courtesy and respect their time.

A practical example is to always arrive on time for meetings and appointments. Develop the habit to arrive for a meeting at least five minutes early and even earlier if you are coming from another location. If you're going to arrive late, contact the meeting's host to let them know you will be late and when you will arrive.

2.8 Technical Management Skills

PMs need additional skills to manage technical tasks for an ES project. These include

Organize projects	Report project progress
Manage Project Schedule	Manage project communication
Manage project teams	Manage budget
Manage problems, issues, and risks	Manage quality
Manage project changes	Manage procurement
Manage project documents	

Organize Projects

The PM, with guidance from the project sponsor, prepares a Project Organization Chart and R&R Chart to inform project teams about their direct and indirect (dotted line) reporting to the PM. The PM establishes guidelines for the project teams' performance for their work. The PM also should provide the organization chart for the project. Chapter 4 describes how to prepare these charts.

Manage Project Schedule

Chapter 4 describes guidelines to create a Project Schedule. Manage the project schedule this way:

- Each week, review the current project tasks with the project team. Follow guides for conducting meetings described above. Focus on progress for current tasks. Each team member should give an update on their progress for their current tasks including:
  - Milestones and deliverables completed
  - "Actual % Complete" (APC) for each task they are working on. The APC is calculated as *actual hours spent thus far/(actual effort) + (estimated remaining effort)*. This formula provides a better estimate of the progress in completing a task and the current estimate for the effort that will be needed to finish a task.
  - Status of effort on CRs and to correct problems, issues, and risks that have been occurred
  - New issues, risks, and CRs
  - Update the Project Schedule weekly to show progress, e.g. hours, new tasks.
- When you modify schedule task, balance the three dimensions for time, cost, and results (The Triangle).

  The task can be modified for one or two of these variables, but not all three. Figure 2.3 shows trade-offs.

- If a change to the schedule baseline is approved, then change the schedule to include approved changes.
  - Tasks and dependencies

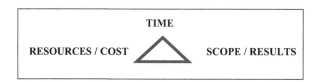

Figure 2.3 Cost – time – results trade-offs.

> – Start and finish dates deliverables, assumptions, resources effort, and other expenditures

■ Change the schedule's version number.

■ If the project becomes seriously behind schedule, the PM can help the team get back on track by holding a short daily meeting (5–15 minutes) to coordinate the team's work and give help to team members. This brief team meeting (often called a stand-up meeting) can be held in person (standing) or by conference call. Team members review
> – what *was accomplished* since the last meeting?
> – what *will be accomplished* before the next meeting?
> – what *are obstacles (issues)* delaying progress?

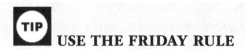 **USE THE FRIDAY RULE**

To help keep the project schedule on track, ask team members to plan their week so they complete planned work on their tasks by the end of day on Friday or alert you so other team members can help them overcome a problem (e.g., user cancels a meeting to complete the requirements for data migration).

Manage Project Teams

The PM's most important responsibility is to direct the project team that will achieve the goals for the project. Here are important practices to help PMs lead an ES project:

■ Review the skills and experience of each in-house team member brought on to the project. The skill levels (junior, experienced, senior, or expert) for team members should match the tasks they will be assigned in the Project Schedule. Outside consultants chosen for the project should have qualifications that match the resources described in the Statement of Work agreement.

- Make sure to arrange with the software vendor a training schedule for project team members. The training will be for developers, technical staff, and ES users in the operation of the ES product.
- Schedule the team's training as a prerequisite before they begin their work for scheduled tasks.
- Hold a separate staff meeting soon after the Project Kickoff Meeting to review the Project Management Plan which covers guidelines for sharing documents, status meetings, handling issues, and action items. This will help the project team to understand your guidelines for their activities.
- Create a shared team calendar to show which days they will be available for onsite or Zoom team meetings. The calendar is useful to show dates when individuals are not working on scheduled tasks, national holidays, vacations, other assignments, and company closings.
- Help the team meet challenges to keep the project on track. These include issues and risks that occur, missed deadlines, CRs, quality issues, technical and business problems, and other roadblocks. The PM can help the team solve business and technical issues by arranging for someone to assist the team who has the expertise in the organization or the vendor.

Manage Onsite and Offshore (OS) Project Teams

If you are using an OS consulting firm to help implement the project's solution, follow these commonsense steps to manage the team:

- Review the resumes submitted for the OS project team members who are assigned to work on your project. Be sure that they have the required technical skills and experience for the project tasks (e.g., senior level skills for bank accounting projects). Also match each resource on the vendors to the list of resources and skill levels given in the approved SOW. Select OS team members who meet your requirements or ask for additional candidates if needed.
- Get a commitment from the OS vendor (in writing if possible), that they will not replace a key member of their OS team for the duration of their effort. This will avoid delays and loss of skills for key members if the vendor wants to move key talent to work on another client's project before yours is completed.
- Establish a schedule to hold progress meetings with the OS team's technical lead and supervisor or on site representative to review progress of the OS teamwork, issues, etc. Issue minutes of these status meetings in a similar way that you would for any progress meeting

with the full onshore team. Include their report as part of the agenda for each full project team meeting.

■ Complete a review of the requirements with the OS team and confirm their approval to deliver the requirements within the approved schedule. This will help to avoid a "surprise" later if they submit a CR for additional effort, time, or cost for not understanding these requirements.

Manage Problems, Issues, and Risks

Issues are problems *that already exist* that must be resolved to avoid missing project deadlines. Risks are unplanned events that *may occur in the future* that can throw off the schedule. The PM must delegate the effort to resolve the issue or risk to someone on the team who will "own the effort". The issue/risk owner will work with team and vendors to investigate and come up with a way to resolve the issue or reduce the impact of the risk.

Here is a basic method to manage project issues and risks:

■ Maintain logs to record and track issues and risks. Allow team members add to logs and update status and other fields.

■ Assign a project team member to "own" the issue or risk and lead the effort to resolve the issue or risk. Assign a priority to each new risk/issue. The owner's assignment should be to research each issue or risk with other team members, investigate and find a way to resolve the issue or reduce the impact of the risk, and then recommend a solution.

■ Track the status for each open issue and risk. Ask the owner assigned to the issue or risk to update the team on their effort to resolve their issue or risk.

Report Project Status

Reporting the progress and recent accomplishments during enterprise systems projects will require different presentations with specific contents and format depending on the group/audience receiving the briefing. If your organization has a standard or frequently used format for these presentations, adapt these to report your project's progress. Figure 2.4

shows a sample of three formats to use to inform the project sponsor, Steering Committee, and other stakeholders. Regardless of the format, these presentations should include the following topics:

- *Status of the work* to implement the new system including the product vendor's team and internal teams. Include Stop Light symbols to show the status of critical tasks for the project and if the schedule is on tract or drifting.
- *Accomplishments and milestones* reached since the last progress report. An updated deliverables list or Gantt Chart can be used to summarize the project's progress.
- *Status of problems and issues* that are still open or were resolved/close since the last review. You can add a demonstration of a function of the ES that is completed.
- *New problems, issues, and risks* that have occurred that may impede progress.
- *Decisions required* to resolve open issues, questions, and CRs.

You may also want to preview your presentation with the project sponsor and other Steering Committee members to get their feedback and support for the outcomes you want from the meeting.

Manage Project Changes

There are several events during a project that may require changes to a project schedule, funding, or deliverables. The organization's goals or requirements may change, budget and spending reductions are required, or the project falls behind, and more resources must be brought in. This process to manage CRs should be included in the Project Management Plan (Chapter 4). Managing these changes will be easier if you follow these commonsense steps:

Require that all CRs are documented and approved using a CR process before the project team proceeds to implement the change. Assign a project team member to "own" the task to evaluate the CR. Their first task is to evaluate the CR information and confirm the project team's understanding of the request.

- Next the CR team should determine scope of the change and give the person requesting the CR an approximate time for the team to evaluate the request.

- The team should estimate the scope of the change and estimate the impact of making this change on the project – work effort, project schedule costs, risks and assumptions used for these estimates.
- The PM should send an email to the CR requestor to tell them that the team can implement the change because it will have minimal impact for the project, summarizing the estimated impact on the project of implementing the change.
- If the change will have a significant impact on the project (schedule, cost, deliverables, risks), the PM should inform the requestor and together submit the CR to the Project Steering Committee for approval.

Manage Project Documents

A PM has the responsibility for all the assets used or created for a project. These include computer equipment, office facilities, tools, organizational assets, and other assets. One of the important assets to manage is the documentation created and used by the project. At the start of a project, the PM should provide guidelines to the team for how these documents are to be controlled and safeguarded.

Here are effective practices to manage the project documents: create, update, use, store, and retrieve.

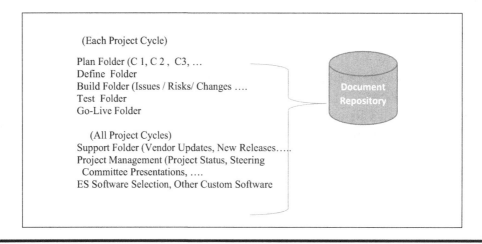

(Each Project Cycle)

Plan Folder (C 1, C 2 , C3, ...
Define Folder
Build Folder (Issues / Risks/ Changes ....
Test Folder
Go-Live Folder

(All Project Cycles)
Support Folder (Vendor Updates, New Releases....
Project Management (Project Status, Steering
  Committee Presentations, ...
ES Software Selection, Other Custom Software

Document Repository

Figure 2.4   Sample organization of project documents repository.

- List document authors initials, names of individuals who created the document.
- Use a standard format for text (font, size), and layout.
- Create a label for the document in a consistent way for subject, author's name/initials, document ID#, and version (number or ID).
- The author(s) are owners of the document. Require that documents are consistently identified, as drafts or approved version
  - date created or modified
  - version number – example 0.1 to 0.9 for draft and 1.0 for approved version
- Document management system (DMS). If your organization has a DMS such as MS-SharePoint or Drop Box, make sure all team members learn how to use it correctly save and retrieve (checkout) versions correctly. Set up security features to control who within or outside your organization has access to project documents. For small projects, the team can set up a central computer repository on a server that is located and maintained by your IT department. Don't allow a team member to maintain a shared file on their personal computer as the project's repository.
- Project files and folders. At the beginning of the project create the project document repository and also create a group of new folders in a logical sequence that will allow the team to maintain documents by subject. Do this at the start of a project to reduce misfiling a document during the project.
- Document approval. If your organization does not have a document approval procedure, specify an approval procedure in the PMP.
- References and work papers. These include physical project documentation including manuals, product literature, blueprints, lab notebooks, test results, and other types of records. The project team should retain work papers and prior versions of these documents for the duration of the project, or a longer time as specified in the organization's document retention Standard Operating Procedure (SOP).

Manage Project Communication

The PM is responsible to set the guidelines for the team's communication with the project team, sponsor, Steering Committee, users, and other stakeholders.

The guidelines should cover emails, texts, online meetings, announcements, presentations, and meetings. The project will run more smoothly if these communications be accurate, concise, and timely. Follow these guidelines:

- *Emails.* Control the volume of emails that flood the inbox team members each day. Ask team members to avoid using "reply all" to reply to you or another team member that will start a long chain of messages about an issue or question. This reduces unnecessary messages that clog inboxes of team members.

 MANAGING A BLIZZARD OF EMAILS/TEXTS

If you or other team members receive a blizzard of emails or text messages each day so it becomes hard for anyone to see which are urgent, ask the team to add the word like "URGENT" or "DECISION NEEDED" in the subject heading to help you spot urgent messages more easily.

- *Presentations.* For a presentation, use the template and format for slides that is standard for the organization. If needed, get an example of a presentation, get a copy from another project. Include slide numbers which makes it easier for the speaker and reader to refer to specific slides. Include a section for backup slides to support slides in main deck. As a rule of thumb, allow two minutes per slide to cover the material shown.
- *Conference calls.* Start a conference call by asking everyone on the call to introduce themselves; first those in the meeting room and then remote attendees. The person taking minutes should record who attends the conference call. Follow other practices to conduct these meetings.
- *Exchange documents between internal and external team members.* Set up accounts on a tool like BOX to allow remote team members to exchange project documents, data files, etc., work with remote

team members or others. Remote consultants, vendor staff, and others should not have access to the team's internal files, documents, or test/production servers.

Manage Stakeholder Expectations

Stakeholders are those who have an interest in your project's outcome. They are typically the managers, project sponsors, and users of the ES within your organization. During the Select and Plan Phases, the PM gets approval from the sponsor and Steering Committee for the charter and scope for the project. However, each key stakeholder often has their own set of goals, objectives, and support for the project. The PM must assess the key stakeholder's support for the project including answering their question: "What am I getting out of my (group's) participation in this project?" or more simply "What's in it for me (WIIFM)?". By the Project Kickoff, the PM should identify the expectations for key stakeholders and determine a plan to meet or change some stakeholders' expectations to get them on board to support the project.

EXAMPLE

Manage Stakeholder Expectations

I was assigned as the PM to lead the implementation of an integrated financial and HR management system for a Fortune 100 company. I began to meet the key shareholders to learn their specific goals and their WIIFM (what is in it for me) expectations.

Before meeting with the VP of Corp HR, I reviewed the current HR system, including the log of problems fixed by the IT support group, and asking the project sponsor (CFO) about the current system's problem areas that could be improved with the new integrated system. I learned the worst complaint with the current system was it was not correctly implemented four years ago and still did not provide up-to-date balances for retirement and 401K benefits for 22,000 employees at HQ and U.S. subsidiaries.

The VP of HR was an ex-marine officer who was a demanding leader and who did not "suffer fools lightly". So, I knew this meeting was going to be a hard sell to get the cooperation of this key stakeholder to support this project and help make it a success.

Before I could start to describe the scope and expected benefits of the new system, the VP of HR interrupted me and asked, "Tell me why I shouldn't toss you out of my office!". He said the IT group had not correctly implemented the current system and it had taken three years and a lot of aggravation to get the current system to operate correctly. He did not trust the IT group to correctly implement any new system.

Because I had learned about the disastrous implementation and weaknesses of the current system, I focused on the benefits the new system could deliver to help his department, and provide his WIIFM benefits. I said I understood the past mistakes and was an experienced PM and would deliver on my promises. The VP agreed to see a demo of the proposed system and invited his staff to attend. At the end of the demo given by the software vendor's staff, he told us that he was convinced this new system could be a major opportunity to improve the company's HR activities.

Soon after, he arranged a "road trip" forms to go to the four US affiliates to describe "his new project" to improve the HR function's computer systems. He became a champion for the project and helped make the project a success.

Manage Project Budget

Preparing and managing a budget for the project is an important skill for all PMs. Each organization (corporate, division, or even a department) will usually have a template and instructions to prepare and approve project budgets. You may need to prepare both expense and capital budgets for the ES project. If your organization doesn't have a form, use a sample from another project.

Manage Quality

Enterprises may have multiple quality assurance (QA) and quality control (QC) requirements for computer systems implemented in different divisions, companies, or functional areas (e.g., R&D, finance, and manufacturing). Therefore, managing QA processes for building and operating ES will be more complex and demanding. PMs need to learn how to manage the processes to ensure the quality of results for their projects. PMs should get familiar with the practices for QA and QC required in their organizations and industry:

- QA refers to the procedures for ensuring the quality in the methods used to create the products, processes, and systems.
- QC is focused on identifying defects in the results completed for the project.

Table 2.4 is a comparison of QA and QC.

PMs should ensure that quality practices established for the project are followed.

Table 2.4 Quality Assurance Versus Quality Control

	Quality Assurance	*Quality Control*
Focus on	QA aims to prevent defects with a focus on the process used to make the product. It is a proactive quality process.	QC aims to identify and correct defects in the finished product. Quality control, therefore, is a reactive process.
Goal	The goal of QA is to improve development and test processes so that defects do not arise when the product is being developed.	The goal of QC is to identify defects after a product is developed and before it's released.
How	Establish a good quality management system. Assess its adequacy. Conform audits of operations of the system.	Finding and eliminating sources of quality problems through tools and equipment so that the stakeholder's requirements are continually met.
What	Prevent quality problems through planned and systematic activities including documentation.	Activities or techniques used to achieve and maintain the product quality, process, and service.
Responsibility	Everyone on the team involved in developing the product is responsible for quality assurance.	Quality control is usually the responsibility of a specific team that tests the product for defects.
Example	Verification is an example of QA.	Validation/software tests and equipment stress tests are example of QA.

There are four important ways to meet quality standards for implementing an enterprise system development:

- Quality standard operating procedures (SOPs)
- Training
- Peer reviews
- QA audits

■ Quality standard operating procedures (SOPs)

If your organization has standard operating procedures for implementing computer systems, the project team will have approved procedures to carry out/perform important tasks such as approving documentation of the ES design, testing the new system before it is deployed, and correcting errors after it is put into use in the enterprise.

■ Training

Ensure that the project team including vendors understands and receives training (if required) in the quality practices to be followed during the project. Distribute copies of the quality SOPs to guide team members.

■ Quality audits

Contact the quality team to review and schedule the times they can conduct an audit of the ES project work. Before the audit, ask for a list of specific mistakes that the quality has found incorrect in reviews of similar projects (e.g., not defining acronyms or technical terms used in documentation). This will help to plan these reviews in the Project Schedule. After receiving the audit results, allow time for the team to correct the deficiencies found in the review. The quality team can revalidate the work.

■ Manage procurement

The PM for an ES system should have training or experience in the basic methods to work with the purchasing group to procure software products, prepare an RFP, and conduct a competitive bid for these services. If you need additional guidance, you might ask a couple of vendors to provide an example of a comprehensive RFP for their ES product, computing service, or consulting service.

While many projects are completed using informal requests for a product or service, a project that requires more complex ES solutions should issue a request for proposal (RFP) to vendors on your short list. The RFP should contain enough information so that bidders can fully understand what is required and expected.

Chapter 3 describes a detailed process to procure an enterprise system solution that will meet your organization's requirements.

2.9 Summary

- A project is a one-time endeavor that organizations carry out to create a unique product, service, or result. Projects have defined start and finish dates, achieve a desired objective, and deliver a required result. However, ES projects can continue through multiple cycles to create an integrated system deployed throughout the enterprise.
- The chapter describes the role and responsibility for six key members of the organization who participate in an ES project deployment. It focuses on the skills, management and technical, that the PM should have to successfully manage (lead) ES projects.
  These key roles for ES project cycles include:
  - Executive sponsor
  - Project sponsor
  - Project Steering Committee
  - PM
  - Project stakeholders
  - ES vendor
- The PM must have two important management skills, business and technical, to lead a large project.

Chapter 3

Choose Enterprise Systems Solution

CHALLENGES DEPLOYING ES

- Assigning project manager who lacks needed skills and experience
- Selecting an ES product that requires more than 10% customization
- Not aligning ES product requirements with organization's LR goals

The selection of an Enterprise System product is the first milestone to implement the ES software system and technology for the enterprise. The project sponsor should appoint a project manager to lead this effort even if an outside consulting firm is hired to conduct the search. As stated in Chapter 1, a decision to select an ES product should come after your organization has developed a strategic plan that defines long-term goals for the organization and objectives for projects for the divisions and operations within the enterprise. The new ES will be built to achieve these goals.

Follow these seven steps to evaluate and select the optimal ES solutions for your organization:

- Organize selection process
- Define high-level requirements for the system
- Identify ES products that match your requirements
- Obtain and evaluate proposals from vendors

DOI: 10.4324/9781003381617-3

- Select the ES package that best meets the requirements for the new system
- Prepare preliminary list of custom changes to the ES software
- Approve ES selection

3.1   Organize Selection Process

To organize a search for an ES product and solution for the firm:

- The project sponsor should send an announcement to inform stakeholders in the enterprise about the study to select an ES product for an integrated information system for the enterprise. This announcement will help stakeholders begin to get onboard to support this project.
- The project sponsor and internal IT management form a small team of internal IT and business members to conduct a search. The Sponsor or the Management Committee may decide to hire an outside consultant to lead this effort and complete this study.
- Keep all documents for this evaluation assignment in a shared computer folder and later move these to the *Project Document Repository* when it is set up.
- Define project plan or timetable to complete the selection effort.

3.2   Define High-Level Requirements

Before the project team can identify and evaluate ES products, they should define the high-level (macro) requirements and features for the new system. For now, they are a guide to evaluate how closely an item of the ES product matches the required functionality of the future system.
These requirements should include:

- Business requirements – These are organization's goals for the ES to help solve the problems defined in the business plan, commission findings, or other document. These functional requirements specify inputs, processes, and outputs for the new system. They could rank by priority (must have, should have, nice to have).

■ Stakeholder requirements – These are functions and features that each stakeholder (department, team, other) wants the system to have to meet their goals to help support the enterprise's business goals.

■ System operation requirements – These are requirements that allow the system to operate correctly including performance, data and access security, and systems administration functions such as maintaining user registration and access privileges. Since most ES products are packaged with supporting tools and services such as security, training, and reporting, the team may not need to define high-level requirements. The Request for Proposal (RFP) can ask for this information.

3.3 Identify Enterprise Systems Products That Match Requirements

The evaluation team begins with an internet search for ES vendors and products for your industry, specific business functions, or target operations that match the scope of your project:

■ Make sure that all relevant documents for this evaluation are collected for each product in a project document library/repository.

■ Identify target ES products for your application and ask each vendor to provide detailed information such as product overview, detailed description, and user manual. The ES product vendor may assign a contact or salesperson who should be able to get the information you need to get a detailed review of the product.

Table 3.1 lists types of information that should be available for your evaluation.

3.4 Prepare Fit/Gap Analysis

The Fit/Gap Analysis Chart is a useful tool to keep track of the information you gather for each ES product. Preparing this chart will help you to compare how closely the features and functions of an ES product match the requirements for your application. Later in the selection process, the feasibility team can use this analysis to compare how products compare to

Table 3.1 Types of Information Useful to Evaluate ES Products

Information	Purpose
ES vendor product publications	Access the vendor's website and publications to learn the product's features and functions; and match them to your organization or industry and business functions. The sources include: ■ Product overview ■ Detailed description ■ User manual ■ White papers – explain some of the features or describe how their product has been designed to meet your unique requirements; a description comparing their product to other similar products ■ Presentations from prior conferences.
In-depth reports from industry research firms	Articles and product reviews and reports for specific ES packages. ■ Industry and Professional Journals – product reviews ■ Technology Research Publications – Gartner, Forrester, or other industry reports.
Remote hosting of ES solution	An ES vendor may offer the option to host your system as an iCloud solution, or at a remote computer center instead of running the system on your organization's computer network. If you consider this option, your operations technical team should evaluate the feasibility of this option, including reliability of the hosting operation, technical support for your system, security of your data, and cost of services.
Product demo	Ask the vendor to provide a demo of their product for the project team. Invite subject matter experts from the business members of the IT organization (QA, systems architect, and other stakeholders). Assign someone from the team to take notes for the presentation, including questions and other information. Ask the vendor to respond to questions.

each other. The Fit/Gap Chart can also show how closely an ES solution compares to the alternative to build a custom solution in-house.

Prepare the Fit/Gap Analysis Chart as a table or spreadsheet with the first column showing a list key requirements and other functions required for this solution including:

- organization functions and workflow requirements
- stakeholder requirements
- technology and infrastructure (database, web, cloud, smartphone)
- security and compliance
- training and other services
- maintenance/support for the ES software including regular software updates to support existing features and new versions for additional features
- the Fit/Gap Chart includes a column with one of the following values for how ES Out-Of-The-Box (OOTB) software matches the requirement:
  - *Fully* meets the requirement or feature when configured
  - *Partially* meets the requirement or feature
  - *Requires workaround* such as a manual procedure or spreadsheet, to meet the required function or feature
  - *Requires modifying OOTB options* to configure settings for this feature
  - *Requires* custom-coded change to the package to provide this feature

Table 3.2 shows an example of a Fit/Gap Chart for an ES package.

Table 3.2   Fit/Gap Analysis Chart

ES Product Name		*Vendor*	
Requirement/Feature	*Description*	*ES Module*	*Fit/Gap*
General ledger account number	GL account number can be two alpha and four numeric	General accounting	C
Customer payment history	Customer payment history for past six months; less history for new customer	Order fulfillment	P

Note:

C – complete; P – requires modification to std configuration; CC – requires custom change; M – requires manual work around.

3.5   Issue RFP and Evaluate Vendor Proposals

Send an RFP to vendors based on your team's review of requirements for the new system and prepare a short list of vendors that may provide the requirements. The RFP process may be assigned to the Purchasing Department of your organization. The purchasing specialist will assist the team in completing this process. First, the team should prepare and issue an RFP to the vendors to prepare a proposal, which describe how their product or service will meet your requirements and provide the best solution for your project.

While many projects are completed using informal requests for a product or service, a project that requires more complex solutions (e.g., changes to a manufacturing facility), should issue an RFP to vendors on your short list. The RFP should contain enough information so that bidders fully understand what is required for their proposal including information about your organization, project scope, required bidder qualifications, timeline, and guidelines for the proposal's format. An RFP should include:

- Description of your organization and mission
- Scope of your new equipment, product, system, or service to acquired and key requirements
- Instructions for preparing the RFP including vendor's response and other required information topics of proposal, customer references, product support (training, maintenance, user groups). This section provides information for submission of proposal (date, address, contacts for their proposal)
- Financial information including pricing of the product's installation, annual maintenance, training, and other services. This information is usually provided in a separate document than the proposal.

Require each vendor agree to sign a non-disclosure agreement if the RFP includes proprietary information about your organization's operations, plans, and so on. Not all vendors you send the RFP will respond. Hold a bidder's meeting within a few days of sending your RFP. This meeting provides each bidder the forum to ask the proposal team (buyer) questions about the required information that the buyer wants all bidders to provide in their proposal. After the meeting, the buyer should promptly answer their questions by responding in writing to all other bidders to allow an even playing field.

MANAGE VENDOR CONTACTS DURING RFP PROCESS

One of the outcomes of the Bidders Conference is also to manage the vendor's contact with your company during the bid process. The lead for the firm's selection team should announce that, to keep all bidders on a level playing field, all vendor questions, meetings with stakeholders, or offers of product demos must be provided to all other bidders. Include the contact information to your organization.

3.6   Select the Enterprise Systems Product That Best Meets the Requirements

When all proposals are submitted, prepare a Product Score Card to evaluate each vendor's proposed solution for the criteria specified in the RFP. Specify the evaluation criteria for each feature and its weight among all criteria. Table 3.3 is an example of a Product Score Card for a vendor's proposal. Narrow the proposals to one or two finalists based on the team's evaluation and score for their proposals.

Table 3.3   Sample Product Score Card

ES Product Name		Vendor		
Feature	*Evaluation Criteria*	*Evaluation*	*Importance*	*Score*
Requirements met	Percentage of requirements met (1–5)	4	60%	2.40
Custom changes required	% of Requirements to customize	3	15%	0.45
Match our standards			5%	
Maintenance/ support			10%	
Security and other factors			10%	
Score			**100%**	

Obtain additional information about the finalists to help make your decision. This can include

- Public records. Check better business records if the vendor has been sued or received complaints from other customers for problems with their installation.
- Product demo. Have the vendor meet with the evaluation team to review their proposals or give a demo of their product.
- Product Roadmap. Review the vendor's Roadmap to learn which new features and services are scheduled for release in the next 12 months
- Training – courses for overview, design, user operation.

3.7   Prepare Preliminary List of Custom Changes

For each finalist, prepare a preliminary list of custom changes to the OOTB features for the ES product that are needed to fully meet your requirements. Include a ballpark estimate to create each custom change. These estimates will be finalized during the project's Definition Phase. The estimate should include

- Requirement(s) that may need a custom feature
- Name of custom feature
- Priority (must have, should have, nice to have)
- Estimate of time and cost to add this feature to the product

3.8   Prepare Business Case and Recommendation

After completing an analysis and comparison of the vendors proposals, the product evaluation team should be able to select the ES product that best meets your project goals.

Begin to negotiate with the winning vendor the price to acquire the product (purchase or lease) and services. This is often called the "Best and Final Price". And the costs to implement the chosen modules of the ES product and custom development of additional feature (fixed fee, hourly rates, or shared costs).

When the evaluation team has made a final choice, the project manager should prepare a recommendation to the Steering Committee including a Product Comparison Chart that compares comparing the evaluation scores for the two (or more) finalists. Table 3.4 is an example.

Second, prepare the Business Case that supports the enterprise proceeding to acquire, implement, deploy, and support the chosen ES package solution. The Business Case should explain *why* this recommended ES solution is the best choice for your enterprise. The evaluation team also can submit a separate report that includes a complete

Table 3.4 Comparison of ES Finalists

		ES 1	ES 2	ES 3
Feature	*Evaluation Criteria*	*Score*	*Score*	*Score*
Requirements can be configured	% Requirements fully met	75%	85%	65%
Requirements needing custom changes	% of Requirements met by customized addition	15%	0%	25%
Requirements can be met by workarounds	% Requirements met by workaround instead of custom change	10%	15%	10%
Total		100%	100%	!00%
Match our technology standards	% ES product software that matches our corporate standards	100%	75%	75%
Maint/support	Quality of vendor support and maintenance services	90% estimate	90% estimate	90% estimate
Security and other factors	% ES product software functions that match our corporate security standards	100%	100%	85%%
Rank Score		1	2	3

set of documents for each vendor's proposal, team's evaluation, and other information.

The Business Case can be part of the presentation to the project sponsor and Steering Committee. It should include the following information:

- Project background
- Key evaluation criteria/requirements for an ES
- Comparison of finalists
- Recommended approach to implement the ES solution
- Business value for proposed solution
- Preliminary project timeline and cost

Check with the Finance Department about how your organization defines the cost (investment) of the product current expense or capital expense), and implementation and capital expense.

Arrange for the vendor to give a presentation and demo of the recommended ES production.

The project team should obtain approval for the choice of ES product and the funding for the project.

The outcome of the Steering Committee meeting should be approval to acquire the recommended ES product.

3.9 Summary

To begin the process, to select an ES product, first form a ES selection team that includes internal systems and technology personnel, project sponsors, and future ES users. Do not rely on outside consultants to conduct this search as they will be biased.

- The search team should prepare a list of goals in the LR plans and strategy and link each goal to objectives for the enterprise to achieve in the next 2–3 years. These objectives can then be linked to the requirements for ES.
- The search team then conducts an RFP to request proposals from ES vendors, evaluate proposals received, and select the ES product that best meets the enterprise requirements.
- The team prepares a Fit/Gap Analysis to identify custom changes to the ES to provide functions that must be added to the ES product. The

team evaluates each custom change to estimate cost and time to create this needed function.

The final step is to prepare a Business Case to implement the selected ES product and present the recommendation to the Steering Committee for approval.

Chapter 4

Plan ES Project

- Over-reliance on outside consulting IT support
- Using current standard implementation method SDLC and not project cycle process for ES projects
- Using current standard implementation process and not project cycle process for ES projects

When the selection of the ES package and funding are approved, the planning for the ES project begins. During this phase, the Project Schedule and other documents are completed and meetings with the project team are held to launch the implementation of the ES. The following planning steps are completed to launch a project. Each of the following documents and events make up the plan phase of a typical systems project; except the scope, complexity, and timeline are much greater for an ES implementation project.

- Prepare project plan documents
- Prepare Project Schedule
- Prepare deliverable log
- Prepare issues/risks log
- Prepare project budget
- Hold the Project Kick-off Meeting
- Begin staffing project

DOI: 10.4324/9781003381617-4

4.1 Prepare Project Plan Documents

In addition to the Project Schedule, the project manager (PM) should prepare five documents that will help guide the project team to meet the project's mission.

Project Charter

The *Project Charter* is a document that describes the project's goals and expected outcomes. For a project to create an ES, this should include additional information including

- project or program name
- project sponsor – for ES projects that will implement modules in multiple phases/project cycles
- project's benefits – summary of expected tangible and intangible benefits plus their link to the organization's goals and plans
- expected period – describe the current estimated time frame to implement ES modules in multiple phases/project cycles
- total estimated costs – including the amount for the current year budget and for additional project cycles.

Stakeholders List

A *stakeholder* is an individual or group who will be affected by the outcome of the project or a decision or activity during the project. Important stakeholders may not participate in the initial project cycle to implement the system; but should be kept up to date if they will participate in a later project cycle.

The ES stakeholder list identifies the people who will have a role in the success of the project. It is important that the PM understands how the ES system's operation and benefits can help stakeholders' support for the project. For example, what is the cost and effort for one shareholder group to replace their current system and switch to the new system? Do they support the expected "switching costs" to adopt the new ES to be deployed to their group?

Preparing this list will help you to think about the different expectations each key stakeholder expects from the project and where you may need to adjust your communication about project progress or issues.

Group / Name	Role / Title	Participation	Expectations
Consumer Products Group (CG)	Director	Approves Budget for Consumer ES apps	Difficulty for CG staff to convert from using current system to new system
Steering Committee (SC)			
SC Member A	project sponsor	Help resolve Issues	Successful Project
SC Member B	VP Finance	Approve Project Budget	Reduce Product Cost 5%
SC Member C	VP Marketing	Define Sales & Mkt requirements	Reduce Overtime 20% except end of Quarter

Figure 4.1   Sample stakeholder list.

Here is a suggested way to prepare this list.

- Start with your enterprises organization chart and learn where group and stakeholder are in the organization and how they are linked to other groups.
- Create a table with stakeholders listed by the group the-y're in (e.g., Steering Committee, technical team, vendor team, etc.). If you need help identifying these stakeholders, ask the project sponsor to provide a contact for a group who will assign the person(s) who will participate.
- For each stakeholder, describe their role for the project: name, project role, % allocated to project contact info, and other useful data.
- For each key stakeholder, find out from the Sponsor or others their history with this project and what specific results they want. Figure 4.1 is a sample of this list.

Project Scope Statement

The *Scope Statement* for an ES project will describe the specific features or attributes of the results (product, process, system, etc.) expected for the project and that the project team(s) intends to deliver. The Scope Statement along with the Charter provide a summary of the purpose and results expected for this project. For most projects this document can be a brief statement of 4–5 sentences.

For ES projects that have an expanded scope, which will be rolled out over multiple cycles, it should include how the scope expands as more modules and custom features are deployed.

The project sponsor and key stakeholders should approve, so they confirm their understanding of the impact of the project on the entire organization and their group.

Project Management Plan (PMP)

The *Project Management Plan (PMP)* are guidelines for team members to follow during this project. It has a different use than a Project Plan or Schedule. It includes guidelines to help the project teams coordinate their effort in a consistent way. A basic PMP should include the following guidelines. Chapter 2 covered the information that can be used for these guidelines.

- Project charter – to provide a description of the project's goals and expected outcomes
- Project organization – project organization chart and R&R chart
- Manage issues and risks – includes guidelines to identify, log, evaluate, take action, track and close issues and risks (Chapter 2)
- Change Control Procedure – a procedure for team members to identify, log, and update the status for issues and risks. Chapter 2 includes a commonsense way to manage change requests
- Manage project documentation – using document management system(s), labeling files, and versions of documents
- Project reporting – weekly status reports, tracking actual hours
- Other guidelines as needed

4.2   Prepare Project Schedule

The *Project Schedule* is the PM's most important tool to manage the activities during the project and bring it to a successful conclusion. It is a guide for the project team to perform their assigned tasks to create and deploy the new system. The schedule for an ES implementation project

should include sections to design, build, test, deploy, support and maintain, and close the current *Project Cycle* and plan for the next cycle.
The Project Schedule should include tasks to define, create, and test at least four key parts of the system.

- Product configuration – Tasks to configure the package usually by the product vendor or outside team specializing in the product. The ES product consultants usually have a starting Work Breakdown Structure (WBS) and estimates for this section of the schedule.
- Custom changes – Tasks to create custom changes to the package usually by the vendor's product development team or in-house IT team. These changes are needed to add required functions to the new ES that are not provided with the OOTB functions of the package.
- Data migration – When you create the Project Schedule, consider starting the data migration (interchange) of legacy data files. Assign a team to start tasks to prepare data to migrate from the legacy systems to the new ES system. The steps to prepare for the data migration are specified in Section 6.7.
- Other systems components – Assign tasks to the in-house or off site teams to implement other requirements including system interfaces, integrated testing, quality checks, and user training.

Here is a standard method to create a Project Schedule.

Create a Work Breakdown Schedule (WBS)

The PM should start to build a Project Schedule by

- Creating a WBS that is a list or sequence of the primary tasks to complete each deliverable completed result for the project
- Divide each primary task to complete the deliverable into subtasks that each should require 1–2 days or less to complete. The result is a list of tasks and deliverable work activities for each project milestone and phase lists tasks to create the key deliverables, work packages, milestones, and other major events for each project phase
- The WBS should include tasks or deliverables that users, consultants, and vendors complete and contribute for the project. The WBS lists the primary tasks and subtasks to create the key deliverables, work packages, milestones, and other key events for each project phase

- The PM, with input from team members, moves through the WBS to define estimates for each task or subtasks
- Duration time (start/finish dates)
- Work effort (hours or days)
- Resource(s) performing the task (title name or initials)
- Predecessor and successor tasks
- Other information to complete the schedule.

A PM usually creates and maintains the Project Schedule, with the help of team members, using project management software, like MS-project, which guides the team through the steps to create the WBS. When the schedule is fully defined, the PM will complete the first draft of a schedule.

Estimate the Duration and Work for Each Task

When the task is assigned to an in-house IT staff, vendor team, or outside ES consultants, the WBS tasks must be planned for the estimated work effort and duration/time to complete.

For each task estimate the effort to complete:

- Estimate the work (number of hours or days)
- Estimate the duration (start and completion dates) to complete the task. If multiple team members work on the task, the total work effort is the sum of the effort for these individuals
- Identify the predecessor task(s) that must be completed before this task starts, e.g., define the effort to build a product after you have completed requirements.

Assign Resources to Each Task

- Start by creating a resource list (people/materials). If you are using a project management software tool, specify the position's title and resource's initials for each resource assigned to a task. Assign more than one resource if needed to complete the task.
- Specify generic names and IDs for each resource/role for the project (e.g. T1 and T2 for Tester 1 and Tester 2). Later, you can add specific

names of the team members assigned to each of the roles for each resource. Specify the number of each type of resource, skill level of the resource (junior, intermediate, senior), and percent of their full-time effort for the duration scheduled for each task.

Estimate Level of Effort for Each Task

There are multiple ways to estimate the level of effort for a tasks. Two of these are the following:

- *Level of effort estimate.* These are estimates by team members or ES consultants who have performed/done the tasks to configure or customize the ES solution before.
- *Three-point estimate.* This is a method for estimating the expected duration by using the average of the estimates for minimum, maximum, and expected effort for a task.

The three-point estimate technique estimates effort to complete a task based on prior experience or best-guesses. The three-point estimate for a task is

- b = the best-case estimate
- *m* = the most likely estimate
- w = the worst-case estimate

The final estimate E (expected value) is then:

$$E = (b + m + w)/3.$$

- *Fixed/target amount of effort.* Some tasks are assigned to complete in a fixed amount of effort. For example, the estimate to approve most project deliverables might be set as 3–5 business days.
- *Task breakdown estimate.* To estimate the effort to complete an into smaller entire task, divide the entire task parts – design, build, and test. Combine the effort to complete each part of the task to get an estimate for the whole task.

Add Status for Individual Tasks

■ Percent complete. Track percent completed for tasks as way to measure progress to complete tasks and verify if there is enough remaining planned effort to complete the task by planned end date

■ Deliverables completed. Use comment field to mark tasks that complete deliverables or work pages (e.g., task that finalizes approval of the Project Schedule)

■ Milestones. To show the completion of key work products or events for each phase

■ Comments. These can include names of deliverable completed with this task and assumptions/explanation that are the basis for estimates for work and duration (e.g., resource skill levels required for the task)

Add Schedule Contingency

Schedule Contingency is the time added (reserved) to the schedule to reduce or buffer the total cost approved for a project. As the project work progresses, the total work effort to complete a milestone or phase may exceed the total effort approved for the schedule.

There are several reasons the actual effort (cost/hours) will exceed the original estimate. These include

■ Steeper learning curve to use new coding tools or data base systems
■ Wrong assumptions for estimate
■ Complexity of custom changes to ES
■ Greater effort to complete configuration, customization, and testing tasks especially if your organization is an early adopter of the ES system
■ Effects of uncertainties or risks for completing certain milestones.

The PM can include this contingency in the schedule by adding one task: to provide a reserve of work hours or days to be used as a reserve bucket to offset the effort that becomes larger than the original schedule. The PM can "draw down" hours to increase the work estimate for tasks that exceed approved estimates. This helps keep the schedule on track for total hours and cost.

Add Section tor Tasks to Manage the Schedule

Include section at the top of the schedule to show the PM's tasks to prepare progress reports for the team and the Steering Committee, help resolve issues and risks, update the schedule and budget, etc.

Review the Draft Schedule and Finalize

After compiling the draft Project Schedule, the PM coordinates send the draft schedule to in-house and contract teams to review. The two best ways to review a schedule are:

- Ask them to use *Reply* and not to *Reply All* to send you their questions, and recommended changes. Combine these suggested
- Hold a team meeting to review the schedule. Proceed through the WBS and discuss each task. Appoint yourself or another team member to keep track of decisions to revise the draft schedule
- Complete the review and approve the final draft schedule with department managers and the Steering Committee.

TIP Some recipients will not have apps to review the draft Project Schedule (e.g., MS-project or MS-project viewer). In this case, circulate the schedule as a PDF format document to stakeholders for their review and final approval.

4.3   Prepare Deliverables, Issues, and Risks Logs

The *Deliverables Log* is a chart that lists all deliverables from the Project Schedule along with start and finish dates and the person responsible for this deliverable. As the project progresses, the PM regularly updates the log to track and report progress in completing these deliverables.

The PM should set up an *Issues/Risks Log* to track issues and risks that may occur during the project.

- An *issue* is a problem that has occurred and will impact the project unless it's solved.
- A *risk* is an event that may occur in the future and impact the project (either in favorite or unfavorite way).

4.4   Prepare Project Budget

Preparing and managing the *Project Budget* for the project is an important responsibility for all PMs. Each organization (corporate, division) will usually have a template and instructions preparing and approving Project Budgets.

You may need to prepare both an Expense Budget and a Capital Budget for a project, with the help of the Financial Department if the organization doesn't have form and instructions for a budget, use a template or sample from another project.

Here is an example to create a Project Budget and track actual vs budget expenditures during the project:

- Create columns for type of expense, monthly budget amounts for each month plus total year, then monthly actual expenses plus a year-to-date total actual
- List expense categories using guidelines from finance or list type of expenses.

4.5   Establish Standards to Build an Enterprise System

An ES is built from multiple applications. Each application is built from modules. The system is created in one or more implementation project cycles. Accomplishing this requires the project teams to use standards to prepare documents, forms, and other artifacts created during a project cycle. Consistently following these standards will yield benefits including:

- Provide standard templates/layouts for documents without the need to create different forms. These standard documents may already exist within the enterprise.
- Approve and file documentation in a consistent way. This will help project teams in the current and future project cycles access documents from earlier project cycles.

Table 4.1   List of Important Standards for ES Projects

Standard	*Purpose*
Document names & ID #	Consistent ID for each form created and used in each ES project cycle
Enterprise name and department name	Identify company (department))
Approvals: Date(s) and signatures	record creator of document
Location of specific data on form Author name	Consistent location of info on form
Document version	Shows version of document. Shows approved version and helps prevent using outdated versions
Names of documents and templates, file names of files, data files, document name and ID number	Unique identifier

- Help project teams, in a different project cycle, more easily reference information from prior cycles
- Help the audit/standards group to conduct a system audit faster (Table 4.1).

4.6   Hold Project Kickoff Meeting

The *Kickoff Meeting* for a new ES project is the event that officially launches the project. The purpose is to give team members, Steering Committee, and other stakeholders an overview of the scope and initial plans for the new project.

The attendees should include key stakeholders for this project, individuals from groups who will contribute to the project (full project team or sub team leads, key stakeholders and support personnel from the departments of Quality, IT, Finance, and other groups). Also invite Project Sponsors, for later implementation cycles, who will lead the later ES project cycles.

The PM prepares the materials for the meeting and hosts the presentations. The agenda for the Kickoff Meeting should include the following topics:

- Introductions of Attendees
- Description of Project: Purpose/Scope/Rational (project sponsor)
- Planned Approach – including Summary Timeline (PM)
- Expected Benefits – Tangible and Intangible (PM)
- Additional Information and Questions

4.7 Begin Staffing Project

The project team will include people from within your organization, outside consultants (onsite, onshore, offshore), and the ES software vendor. These groups usually assign their members to fill positions for resources for the Project Schedule. Therefore, the PM is not given the responsibility to choose (recruit) project team members. When team resources are made this way, the PM should confirm the qualifications and availability of each assigned person.

Internal Staff

The PM should request that the IT department and other internal groups assign resources to the project. If the IT group cannot assign all the technical staff needed, then the PM should obtain staff that is available with different skill levels. If key resources are not available full time, arrange for stakeholders to assign (commit) their staff members for part of each month to on work on scheduled tasks.

The PM, with the help of the project sponsor, should request that groups within the enterprise assign individuals to work on the project to perform tasks that require user participation including project meetings (Kickoff and status) and preparation of system requirements (using Deep Dive method).

Outside Team

When the ES project Schedule requires resources from the ES vendor or a software consulting firm, the PM should interview and verify that recommended technical staff have experience configuring and customizing the current version of the ES product. The PM will need to approve a *Statement of Work (SOW)* for the firm's effort. It is important to include a warranty in the SOW that the vendor will keep resources to the project for a specific time after the launch of the new system (a month or more) to correct defects and problems which occur after the new system begins deployment (goes Live). The warranty should be set based on the complexity of the ES solution (number of modules). Other factors will increase custom changes. If your organization is an *early adopter* of this product, estimate the contingency cost and schedule for this project.

Obtain Resources to Support Project Staff

Before the project team begins their work, the PM should arrange for the office space, IT, and other resources to support the team. These resources include:

- Office space that allows the team to be near each other.
- Meeting room(s) for the team to hold meetings, work together on tasks, meet vendors, etc. The PM or team members may want to reserve a team meeting room in advance for recurring meetings or other events with stakeholders and vendors.
- Project team contact list. The list will help the PM and team members to know who is on the team, their role, and their contact (phone, email, and office location).
- Project document repository. Should be organized by subject. Team members should maintain their draft and competed documentation in the project repository. Chapters 2 and 4 cover the basics for setting up a computerized document repository.
- Training. Before starting to perform work, the project staff need training in the functions and features of the ES product and other software they will use to implement. Your organization may also require training (and certification) to handle controlled documents, validate complete software, and other SOPs. The PM should contact another PM or a member of the IT quality group to find out which training is required. Identify required training as scheduled tasks in the Project Schedule and an expense in the Project Budget.

Table 4.2 Key Tasks Performed, Documents/Deliverables Prepared, Methods and Tools Used

Key Tasks	Deliverables	Methods/Tools

Prepare project documents	Project charter
	ES project stakeholders
	project management plan
		■ Use templates and samples
		■ Identify ES project stakeholders
		  – Enterprise org charts
		  – project sponsor

Prepare project schedule	Project schedule	■ Work breakdown structure
		■ Task effort estimate techniques
		  – Level of effort
		  – Three point
		  – Fixed amount of effort

Prepare deliverable log	Deliverable log`/chart	Project schedule
Prepare issues/risks log	Issues log Risks log	Assign issue/risk owner
Prepare project budget	Project budget	Financial department instructions Spreadsheet software
Project kickoff meeting	Kickoff meeting presentation	Business case presentation software
Begin staffing project	Project organization chart	Staff resumes Consulting firm SOW

4.8 Summary

The chapter describes the key tasks to perform, documents/deliverables to be prepared and approved, and methods and tools used (Table 4.2).

Chapter 5

Design ES Solution

CHALLENGES DEPLOYING ES

- Lack of business leader's commitment and continuous support
- Failure to set realistic goals for ES based on long-range plans
- Choosing ES product that requires more than 5% customization

This chapter describes a new method called a *Deep Dive* to define the requirements for a new system. The process is very different and easier than for a system for just one or two corporate operations. The prevalent method designs all the functions and features from the beginning (the ground up). The new method starts with a guided tour of features, functions, and data values delivered with the downloaded ES software from the vendor.

5.1   Design Enterprise Systems Solution

The design for an ES requires a very different process called the *Deep Dive* because most of the core functions and features you want for the new system have already been researched, designed, tested, and included in the Out-Of-The-Box (OOTB) software from ES vendor. The process begins

DOI: 10.4324/9781003381617-5

69

when the enterprise designates an internal team of IT systems analysts or consultants to prepare the functional requirements. The steps are as follows:

- The design team meets in a conference room that is reserved for multiple sessions. The team receives a notebook to write notes for each module as the presenter shows how each part of the application is reviewed.
- The vendor's presenter explains how the Deep Dive sessions will help the design team develop the requirements.
- The presenter begins each session by answering questions from the prior session. They then proceed through the screens for each task of the application of the OOTB programs. The navigation of the software is in the same order that the users would process a transaction.

They are included as *Out-Of-Box (OOB)* functions of the ES system. The direct way to finalize the detailed requirements specifications for the new system is to adopt these OOB functions and features for the new system and then identify missing functions that need to be added as custom coded or included as a workaround manual procedure. This method is called the *Deep Dive*.

An enterprise designates an internal team of IT systems analysts or consultants to prepare a detailed *Functional Requirement Specification (FRS)* and *Technical Requirements Specification (TRS)* for the new system design. The team can prepare these specifications using the results of their Deep Dive.

The new functions that are needed can be developed with a standard method like:

- *As-Is and To-Be design document* the functions of the current system(s) (As-Is) then design a new system (To-Be) that has improved functions, features, and technology.
- *Joint Application Design (JAD)*: This is a method to collect business requirements for developing a new information system by conducting collaborative work sessions with IT and system users.

- A *function* describes *what* the procedure, process, product, or machine will accomplish to meet a goal or objective. Example: input tasks, calculations, or outputs.
- A *feature* is a tool that describes *how* the function is accomplished. Example: display menus, drop down lists, next/previous page actions.

5.2   Define Requirements for Configuration

The *Deep Dive* is a method that will help the project team define the detailed requirements for an ES system without having to start the design from a blank page using the more difficult methods (As-Is/To-Be, JAD, or others).

Follow these steps to conduct a Deep Dive into your new ES system:

- Assemble a team of system users, developers, and other stakeholders to participate in a detailed demonstration of the software. The Deep Dive review should also include members of support groups (security, operations, Help Desk, and training). The purpose of this detailed review is to confirm the detailed requirements for the new system. You may want to have a separate walk-through for each module of the ES product.
- Choose someone to take notes of the project team's comments and questions for each session.
- The Deep Dive facilitator guides the team through a detailed review of the ES product operation including transactions, display screens, administrator functions, security controls, standard reports, and other features. The design team discusses how closely each of product's functions and features match the requirements for the new system. The ES functions that are accepted become the initial design for the configuration of the new system.
- The design team also identifies the requirements that are not included in the ES product. During the Deep Dive walk-through, which may require multiple sessions, the design team chooses which OOTB functions match the functions required for the new system. The design team also identify additional options (custom change, workaround) to meet the requirements missing from the ES solution. The final list of the customized functional requirements is included in a Functional Requirements Specification (FRS).
- Conduct each Deep Dive session using meeting software such as Zoom. Consider providing each attendee a packet or three-ring binder for screen shots for all the transactions and functions of the system. This will help participants to write notes during the review.
- During the walk-through, attendees can record their questions, comments, and other notes about how these OOTB functions and

transactions will meet the requirements for the new system, including making changes to reflect the organization's unique requirements (e.g., layout of a screen).

■ Changes can be added to a "parking lot: list to list changes discussed".

■ When the team finishes their review, the person taking notes collects the notes from everyone and organizes suggestions, questions, description of custom changes, and other ideas.

■ The ES design team evaluates the results of the workshops and
– Gets answers for vendor's questions
– Confirms which of your required features are feasible for vendor's proposal

TIP During the review of the ES system, users of their current computer system or process may want to modify the new system to mimic the existing system. They may want to perform their work the current way and avoid having to learn a new way to perform this work. The PM will need to be alert for the request to change an OOTB function, so it mimics the current system. For example, the cost for the user team to prepare a year-end report may be ten workdays of their effort; but the ES project team's estimate to create a custom routine to produce this report is 18 days.

5.3 Define Requirements for Custom Changes

Follow these commonsense steps to evaluate the best way to manage the need to create custom changes to the "OOTB" features of the ES system you are implementing.

Prepare an Analysis of Custom Changes

Prepare the analysis of the impact and cost for the custom changes needed for the new ES system. Review the list of custom changes to the ES software that were identified during the initial feasibility study. This analysis should include estimates of the cost, risk, time, and resources needed for each custom change. These will add up to show the impact of this custom change on the project schedule and budget. Review this analysis with the project stakeholders and set the priority and decide if there are alternates for each proposed custom change:

- High – must have
- Medium – should have
- Low – nice to have

Minimize the Need for Custom Changes to the ES Software

Before starting to define the specifications for a custom change to the ES system, look for alternatives to avoid having to create a custom-coded feature.

If there are requirements or features for your solution not provided in the ES product's OOTB functions, the PM should coordinate an evaluation of alternatives to provide the missing feature before creating a custom software change. The ES vendor should provide a *Product Roadmap* that describes the timetable for new features or services planned for future releases of their product. Arrange a conference call or meeting between members of your project team and the vendor's product support team to discuss how future additions to the product might support your requirements.

There are several ways to avoid customizing a ES product. These are described in Table 5.1.

Design Custom Changes to ES Software

The Project Management Plan should include guidelines or standards for the design of custom features. These should include:

- Design standards
  Define a set of design standards for custom changes to the ES package. These guidelines will simplify the effort by the in-house and ES project team to design, develop, and integrate custom changes. These design standards include:
  - Guidelines already established for OOTB features such as names of tables, transaction IDs, etc.
  - Standards to create changes to parts of the ES product such as report formats or error messages reports, interfaces with other systems.

Table 5.1 Options to Avoid Custom Changes to ES Products

Options	How	Pro	Con
1. Define temporary or permanent workaround to avoid the need for a custom-coded change	■ Implement a manual step in place of an automated process ■ Change the process to eliminate the step	■ Avoid need to modify ES software ■ Implement system faster ■ Lower implementation cost	■ Organization must change current practices ■ May reduce efficiency of new system
2. Defer creating the custom change until a later release of your new system	Modify project schedule	■ May simplify a process and increase productivity ■ Avoid need to modify the ES software for first release ■ Implement system faster ■ Lower implementation cost for first release	May need to implement a temporary workaround
3. Get the vendor to agree to jointly create the custom change for your initial system release and then add it as a standard product feature in future release	Get agreement that vendor will develop the custom change for your initial system release; and then add it their Product Roadmap as a standard product feature in a future product release	Avoid need to modify the ES software and maintain change in-house Lower future support cost	Cost for creating this new feature

Table 5.1   (Continued)

4. Find workaround until vendor includes the needed function in a planned future product release	Product Roadmap must show this future addition and its priority and estimated release date	■ Avoid need to modify the ES software ■ Implement system faster	■ You may need to customize the ES application to maintain your competitive advantage ■ May need temporary workaround
5. Find another software product (bolt-on) that provides the needed requirement and integrate it with the ES system	Find another SOW product that provides a needed function (e.g., data security) and create an interface to the ES software	■ Avoid need to modify the ES software ■ May implement system faster ■ May lower implementation cost	Cost of additional software

- Defining requirements for system interfaces.
- Custom-coded programs needed to create a link to exchange data between the new ES-based application and other systems in the organization.
- Reports.

ES systems and modules usually include a group of functions or a reporting module functions to prepare printed or online reports and data analyses (query, spreadsheets, charts) for end users of the new system. One commonsense approach to define the group of reports and other outputs for the new system is to first review all reports provided by the current system. Next, decide which of these reports should be prepared with the new system. The matching OOTB reports provided by the basic ES software may not report data exactly like the current reports (e.g., show data with decimal places). During the configuration of the ES software, simple changes can be made to reports so they present results that match the prior system. Requirements for reports that aren't provided by the ES package should be defined and added to the group of custom changes for the new system.

TIP You will need to maintain programs from your current (legacy) systems to access data files which are not migrated to the ES. These programs will be used to prepare regular and ad hoc reports and queries (e.g., at year-end) after the new ES has been deployed.

Approve Custom Changes

A separate decision will be needed to approve the specific choices and budget for a slate of custom software changes to the ES software for the initial release for your system. This decision can be made after ranking these changes:

- Define priorities and alternatives to implement each custom change
- Evaluate options to avoid custom changes
- Estimate cost to implement each custom change

5.4   Define Requirements for Data Migration

Separate programs will be needed to convert and transfer data from the organization's existing (legacy) systems to the new ES system. Chapter 6 describes the method to convert data from an existing (legacy) system to the new ES system.

5.5   Prepare System Technical Requirements Specification

The system architect should prepare and obtain approval for the TRS for the ES. The in-house computer operations group creates the design for the system architecture for the new system (Table 5.2).

Table 5.2   The Tasks, Deliverables, Methods/Tools to Define Design

Key Tasks	Deliverables	Methods/Tools
Define ES configuration requirements	ES configuration requirements	Table function of MS Word or other tool to create tables
Define additional requirements to customize ES	List of ES custom changes	Table function of MS Word or other tool to create tables
Prepare Requirements Traceability Matrix	Requirements Traceability Matrix Form	Table function of MS Word or other tool to create tables
Define requirements for data migration	Data migration table	Table function of MS Word or other tool to create tables
Define system architecture	■ Technical requirements specification ■ System architecture diagram	Draw in MS PowerPoint or other tool for diagrams
Revise project documents	Revise schedule, budget, and other documents	Table function of MS Word and Excel or other similar tools

5.6 Prepare Requirements Traceability Matrix

The *Requirements Traceability Matrix (TM)* is used to manage the building and testing of all requirements for the new application. It is a list of requirements the ES project teams will follow. Each requirement for an ES module is listed and identified by

- reference ID
- description of the requirement feature
- reference to the location (module, transaction, or function) in the ES system
- type of function (configured, customized, integration, interface to another package or system)

Figure 5.1 is a sample of the Traceability Form.

If the ES vendor has a TM for the OOTB requirements provided for the ES software, use this as a starting point to prepare the complete TM for your new system. Add requirements to each component (input, processing, output, data management, reporting) that will be custom additions to the system.

	Functional Requirement Spec		Design Spec	System Test	User Acceptance Test
R#	Req #	FRS	Spec #	System Test #	Script #
1.	1-1	Launch Application	1-1 open from home screen 1-2 1-3	ST-1.1	UAT-A-01
2	1-2	Log into Application	2-1 2-2 2-3	ST-2,1	UAT-A-02
3.					
4.					
5.					

Figure 5.1 Traceability Matrix Form.

5.7   Revise Project Schedule and Budget

When the new system's requirements and design are completed, the PM should revise the project schedule, budget, and other documents and get approvals for the completed design.

5.8   Summary

The design for an ES requires a very different process because of the scope of the core functions and features for an enterprise. The second reason is the functions and interface of multiple applications are prebuilt and tested. They are included as OOTB functions of the vendor's ES software.

Chapter 6

Build and Test Enterprise System

CHALLENGES DEPLOYING ENTERPRISE SYSTEM

- Selecting an ES product that requires more than 10% customization
- Using current standard SDLC method and not Project Cycle process for ES projects
- Assigning project manager who lacks needed skills and experience
- Not using a buffer for costs and schedule over budget

This chapter describes the steps to build and test a new ES application. Building an ES application for an enterprise starts by configuring most of the programs the vendor delivers as Out- of- the-Box (OOTB) functions and features. If you have chosen an ES product that meets most of your requirements, then there is much less of a need to customize or add other software. A system is made up of multiple applications. Each application consists of functional modules that are built in one or more *Project Implementation Cycle(s)*. There are five key parts required to build each module that makes up of the application – configure, customize, migrate legacy data, prepare system interfaces, and install additional software packages.

DOI: 10.4324/9781003381617-6

I BUILD THE SYSTEM

6.1 Configure OOTB Functions

After your organization loads the OOTB software to your development computer platform, a team (on-premises or outside/offshore) configures this starting version of *modules* for the new system. These include functions that the vendor's product research team provided for the basic module. The product vendor usually assigns a team to configure and test OOTB components of the ES software; these modules have been prebuilt and tested to be implemented for a specific module for the new system.

The ES vendor team usually works at a remote site that is either onshore or offshore. The organization's on site team uses their own development computer which has been configured to be compatible with the enterprise's development computer system.

There are two ways the ES vendor provides the starting application software to the customer:

- downloaded to the customer premises or
- downloaded from the ES vendor's database maintained on their own site in the *cloud*.

The process to build the new system (Project Cycle) has phases that are similar to the standard system development process (SDLC) for older system, but have different steps to build and test modules of a new enterprise system:

- *Customize*: For OOTB functions that cannot be configured to provide required functions, the team must add code to modify the module to the functions needed. The changes may be a small modification to OOTB programs or larger new coded routines.
- *Configure*: Most of the modules delivered for your ES are pre-coded and tested OOTB functions. Configuring the software requires choosing options for functions, such as checking for the minimum/maximum values allowed for data tables.
- *Legacy data* (tables, records) imported or exchanged with other internal or external data.
- *Interfaces with other systems:* Interfaces between existing internal legacy systems and the matching data tables used by the new system. Interfaces between outside systems also may be a requirement.

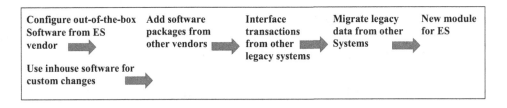

Figure 6.1   Building an ES system module.

Figure 6.1 is a view of the components to build to create a system module.

6.2   Customize OOTB Functions

Some prebuilt functions and features delivered for the ES module will
not match the requirements for the client's system. These custom changes
provide requirements that are not met in the current version of the ES
product. These custom changes are usually developed by the vendor's team
who have more knowledge of the delivered software.

The vendor or client may know of another software product that can
provide the needed functionality without changing the OOTB software. This
separately acquired software is a "*bolt-on*" to the ES module to eliminate the
need for customized changes.

For example, a workflow function may be available OOTB to approve
a special customer order. It may be included to allow the special request
to go "up-the-chain" of management to approve this order. The required
workflow must be customed to change the workflow to skip one level, that
is, go around one required approval step.

6.3   Modify Legacy Data and Migrate to the New System

Before starting to modify the legacy system, data, and migrate it to the
new system, the team should obtain a sample of the legacy data and the
results from possessing this sample. You need to ensure the legacy data is
up-to-date, accurate, cleansed, and matches the format of data for the new
system. Here is the process:

- Assign a team to evaluate the match between the legacy data files
  to the same files of the new ES system. The team should include

individuals from departments who are designated as "owners" of each legacy data file and members of the development team.

■ This team meets to examine the definition of data fields, data field format, and errors for the content of legacy data fields that must be "cleansed" before they are migrated to the new system. The team then makes the needed changes. Changes include:

- Adjust the definition of fields to match definition for new files, e.g., A/N to numeric only
- Add data values to fill blank fields in the legacy records to new system
- Change data fields in legacy system to match the length of data record in new system, e.g., add zeros to front of longer fields in new system
- Change value of legacy data to match the standard values for this data in new system, e.g., coke or Coca-Cola to Coca Cola.

The team also prepares a program to transfer this legacy data to the new system and verify it is correctly modified and migrated.

6.4 Prepare Programs for Systems Administration Functions

The ES product includes software programs to provide system administration functions for your new system. The programs included with the ES software help the system administrator perform these functions. These include:

■ Register new users
■ Set permissions to access data
■ Run backup and recovery of results of the system tests for the new modules and test data and keep it off site
■ Exchange data between the legacy system and the new system
■ Implement internal security procedure such as backup/restore of new system.

II TEST THE SYSTEM

The steps to conduct the systems test for the new application are:

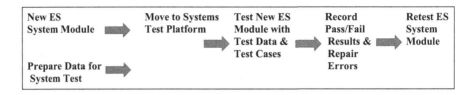

Figure 6.2   System test for a new ES system module.

- Prepare Test Plan
- Assemble Test Team
- Setup integrated testing environment
- Prepare Test Plan
- Train Test Team
- Conduct systems test
- Fix defects and retest
- Move new application to the production platform.

Figure 6.2 shows the steps to perform the *System Test* for the new application modules.

6.5   Form Test Team

The PM designates a *Test Coordinator* to manage the testing of the application modules. The PM and heads of business groups assign individuals from their staff to the Test Team. Individuals on this team should not test components that they built. Instead, other team members will test these components.

6.6   Prepare Test Plan and Calendar

- The Test Coordinator, with members of the *Test Team*, creates the *Test Plan*. The team starts with the Requirements Traceability Matrix for the functions to be tested. Refer to Chapter 4 for guidance preparing the Requirements Traceability Matrix. Another source for a Test Plan is to use the ES vendor's generic test plan and test scripts for each of the application modules.

- The Test Plan includes
  - Form the Test Team
  - Set up systems test platform
  - Convert and migrate legacy data
  - Prepare test cases
  - Test system
  - Correct errors and retest
- The Project Coordinator (PC) and the computer operations manager schedule the dates for the operations group to setup the test platform.
- The team prepares the *Test Data* to use for the systems tests.
- The PC is responsible to maintain a *Test Calendar* which includes the dates to start and complete the key steps for Test Team to conduct the systems tests, correct test errors, and then retest. The dates in the Test Plan should include an estimate to correct errors and perform a second and third round of testing. The computer operation's schedule must provide for dates when the operation's group will limit the availability of the test platform because of other priorities including processing quarter and annual business results, business holidays, and other events.

6.7 Setup Systems Test Platform

As noted in Chapter 4, setting up the testing platform should be completed before the test team starts to move the completed modules and test data to the test platform.

The computer operations group is responsible for setting up the test platform. The PM contacts the head of operations when the team needs a platform for production testing.

The in-house and outside teams may use separate computer platforms to complete their parts of the ES module. Then all parts are transferred and combined on the enterprise's test platform. During the design phase, the system architect prepares an architect design for the production computer components and network to use when the new system goes live and starts production.

Any problems of compatibility between the development computer systems used for building and the in-house system Test Platform (computer, data base, and programming software) must be solved before the new system modules can be system tested. The development team may need to obtain help from the in-house system engineers or the ES software vendor to help to resolve these issues.

6.8 Prepare Test Data and Cases

- Select sample of legacy system data files and the results (transactions, updated records, and reports) for processing this data with the legacy systems.
- Prepare the *test data* for the systems test the ES modules for the application.
- Process the legacy system and use the modified legacy files for testing the the new system.
- Modify the legacy data (Section 6.5) to match the format of the new system and migrate the files as *Test Data* for the system tests for the new system.

Members of the Test Team prepare a series of Test Cases. *A Test Case* is a written document that includes the steps to test the functions of an ES software product. The tester performs these steps to determine if the functionality is partially or completely fulfilled. A Worksheet (Excel) or Table (Word) can be used to create a Test Case. The Test Case should include the following facts information:

- ES application software component name
- Test Case ID – Traceability Matrix ID or test script ID
- Test Case description – Description of steps
- Assumptions
- Preconditions
- Test data used
- Expected result
- Actual result
- Status – Pass/fail
- Comments
- Signature and date of tester

6.9   Train Test Team

User training is essential in encouraging your workforce to engage with their new ES system and not fall back on their legacy system or develop workarounds. You can only realize the full potential of an ES system if people have adequate training.

The Test Plan schedule should include tasks to train the test team; so each member of the organization understands the basic functions, transactions, and operation for the new ES modules they use including navigation of screens, transactions, and other parts of the application.

Vendor proposals (Chapter 3) should include information about their training classes.

6.10   Conduct System Tests

Figure 6.1 shows the steps to build ES modules for new ES. Figure 6.2 shows the steps to transfer the new application modules and test data to the Test Platform for the team to begin testing systems for the new application. The testing of the application follows these steps:

- The Test Coordinator maintains a Log of Test Cases including assignment to Test Team members for each round of testing, test results, correction of errors, and retesting.
- Each Test Team member performs the test cases assigned to them. They complete the form to indicate which steps were completed successfully or not and include the results.
- The team member completes the information for each test cases to record the results of the test including pass/fail, updated displays, output report, and printed or digital copy of results (labeled with the Test Case ID).
- At the completion of assigned Test Cases, the team member sends their set of Test Cases to the Test Coordinator.

6.11   Fix Defects and Retest

- For each round of testing, the Test Coordinator collects the completed Test Cases, logs results, and manages the correction of errors.

- They maintain a Log of Test Cases including dates assigned, completed, correction of errors, and schedule to retest Test Cases after repair of the application module.
- Members of the Test Team correct the application errors that caused a test failure, report progress, and retest a Test Case after the errors are corrected.

6.12   Compliance Test for ES Systems

For some enterprises, there are regulatory, government, and audit requirements for the manufacture, distribution, and sale of regulated products like drugs and medical equipment and other regulated products. The purpose of *Compliance Testing* for ES systems is to certify that the software, instruments, and processes used to produce regulated products are compliant with industry requirements. This type of testing can be expensive and time consuming.

Many ES vendors have prepared compliance tests for their software which their customers can acquire and use. As part of the agreement for acquiring an ES package, the project team or procurement office should look into this option and negotiate this additional feature.

The Test Team acquires or prepares the test cases to conduct and tests to show that the software and hardware configuration will repeatedly produce the results expected for the regulated product.

6.13   Summary

This chapter describes the steps to build and test an ES.

The steps to build four components of the application module:

- *Configure* – Install the OOTB functions. The development team configures the ES application by using a group of screens (displays) with the development computer. You may assign the task to the vendor team as they have experience and skills to configure the ES product. The ES vendor team usually works at a remote site, using their own computer, to create and test this task. Verify their computer infrastructure is compatible with the enterprise's computer infrastructure.

- *Customize* – Create custom functions not provided OOTB in ES product. The in-house team creates changes to customize functions that are not available with the OOTB product. An alternative is to assign the vendor's consulting team to build and test these custom functions.
- *Integrate* – Prepare programs to integrate the new system with other ES.
- *Data migration* – Modify data from other internal or external legacy systems to match format of data for new system.

The steps to test the ES:

- Set up integrated testing environment
- Train Test Team and conduct system tests
- Conduct integrated tests.

Chapter 7

Deploy the Enterprise System

CHALLENGES DEPLOYING ES

- Lack of business leader's commitment and continuous support
- Ignoring common ES application dependencies with other systems
- Failure to adequately train users of the New System

This chapter describes the steps to deploy a new ES application. These tasks are:

- Complete go-live preparation
- Plan deployment
- Train uses of the of the new application
- Plan support
- Train support team
- Deploy new application
- Monitor deployment

7.1   Complete Go-Live Tasks

The tasks to complete before the go-live event include confirming that the computing resources and backup procedures are ready for operating the

DOI: 10.4324/9781003381617-7

system. The go-live begins by moving the application to the enterprise's production computing environment. Other tasks include:

- Complete pre-go-live application and testing
- Confirm required network, reliability availability, and speed
- Confirm computer resources are allocated, including databases, online and off line storage capacity
- Confirm the Backup procedures to offline facilities are accurate

7.2   Prepare Deployment Plan

The *deployment* of applications for a new system requires careful planning and organization because things will seem a little chaotic until the deployment is completed. During this roll out, legacy systems may be down, new applications will have software problems, commitments for time, budget, and assigned staff may be exceeded. It is essential that the project manager and the deployment team know at least weekly who's working on current tasks, status vs schedule, and updates for new and open problems or issues and who owns the correction of these problems. It is important to communicate any plans that may impact the wider organization.

The tasks to prepare for the deployment will vary for each organization:

- Small enterprises may have one or two locations to implement an entire system and can complete deployment in weeks.
- Midsize enterprises have multiple locations and divisions to adopt the new application(s). Their deployment could take months.
- Large enterprises will deploy their application and system in multiple project cycles. Their deployment could take years to complete.

The following tasks are included the deployment plan.
Prepare a schedule for the enterprise sites that will implement the new application:

- Each department or location appoints a *Super User* from their group to help prepare a deployment plan and help roll out the application in their group.

- The implementation team develops a schedule to install the new application for each all groups and users. The schedule should adjust for dates when the staff is not working (holidays, vacations, year-end, and other peak periods). The nonworking days will vary for each country.
- The schedule should include a buffer for additional hours that can be added to tasks that require more time than planned, especially for the first or second project cycle.

7.3 Communicate to New Users and Wider Audience

- Create a communication plan for the go-live activities including emails and staff meetings
- Prepare communication to the wider organization if their activities may be affected during the deployment
- Update the contact data for all users and support staff

7.4 Set Up Support and Help Desk

With the new application in production and ready to deploy, the IT organization should proceed to set up the support for the application. This activity includes:

- Help Desk – to assist users in their tasks using the system
- Software maintenance group – fix software errors, manage installation of updates from vendor
- Application downtime – procedure to notify users and provide quick response, repair source of the problem
- Computer resource usage – maintain the required database size, internet speed, mainframe, or sever capacity for volume of transactions
- Security – intrusion, block unauthorized users
- Backup and recovery of data

7.5 Train Users

There are two groups to train before the start to deploy the application.

- system support
  - database administrator
  - software maintenance team that corrects errors and installs later versions of the application
- new users
  - Super Users
  - Regular Users

The ES vendor or consultant, who helped build the application, should be your first choice to conduct this training and provide user guides for new users. The training can be conducted on site or offsite using Zoom. A Super User in the group should help individuals who have difficulty navigating the new application.

Following their training, users should demonstrate they can correctly use the application to process transactions.

7.6   Launch Deployment

Announce Launch of New Application

About 2–3 weeks before the start of the deployment, the project sponsor sends an announcement that the new application will start to be rolled out and the schedule for the implementation at sites (dates, team member assigned to help end users to use the new application, and other important information). The project manager can also follow up and hold a meeting to discuss and answer questions about the deployment. The ES vendor or consulting firm can help to prepare the materials for the meeting (PowerPoint presentation and handouts).

Deploy New Application

The following are basic ways to manage the deployment:

- Follow the approved schedule; but first implement the application at a small number of locations to identify and fix any kinks in their implementation.
- Before starting the deployment of the new application at each site, contact the manager of the department, site, or group for feedback

about the staff's training, readiness, and concerns about switching to use the new ES application.

7.7   Monitor Deployment

- The deployment team should maintain a log of the tests that failed and the adjustments made. This log will help the team report the status of the rollout.
- The deployment team reports monthly how well the deployment is going. The team also reports results achieved such as reduced cost of raw materials inventory or the cost of overtime hours.
- Report the results (success and problems) for deploying the application (software) and implementation at sites.

7.8   Summary

This chapter covers the steps to deploy the ES and support it.

- After the team completes the integrated testing for remaining high-priority items, the deployment team launches the installation of the new ES.
- The deployment plan includes the tasks such as issuing the schedule and training end users, and to keep senior management and department managers informed about the deployment team's progress.
- The deployment team should maintain a log for each location of positive and negative events and adjustments made. This log will help inform later deployment teams of issues that may occur for their deployment plan.
- When the new applications are fully implemented, the deployment team should report estimated benefits the new applications will provide (e.g., reduced cost of materials for a manufacturing enterprise or increased donations for a non profit organization).

Chapter 8

Close Enterprise System Project Cycle

8.1   Introduction

Once the new system deployment has been completed, the Help Desk and software support team should be ready to correct software problems for the new system and install new releases of the ES vendor's software.

The tasks to complete and close the project cycle include closing contracts with vendors, reporting project results to the Steering Committee and other stakeholders, completing a report for lessons learned during the project, and completing and filing the remaining project documentation. The key tasks to close the ES project are:

- Archive Project Documents
- Close vendor Contracts
- Submit Project Reviews
- Begin Planning for Next Project Cycle

DOI: 10.4324/9781003381617-8

8.2   Archive Project Documents

The tasks to complete the project document archive include:

- The project manager (PM) sets a deadline for team members to complete their project documents/deliverables, obtain the required approvals, and move them to the project document archive. This task should be confirmed by feedback to the PM.
- The PM completes the final version of the deliverables log.
- Project team members complete final versions of project documents they are responsible for, get required approvals, and save them in the project archive by the target date.
- Team members, including consultants, need to move required documents from their desktop hard drives to the Project Document Archive before they leave the project.

8.3   Close Vendor Contracts

Before the contracts with vendors can be closed, they must complete their assignments and deliverables. Their final invoice(s) should then be promptly approved and submitted to your Finance Department (Accounts Payable). A final payment should be withheld until the vendor performs all their tasks specified in the contract or SOW including support during a warranty period.

8.4   Submit Project Review

The PM presents two important reports about the results of the project:

- Final report to Steering Committee to summarize the results of the team's effort to roll out the new system, benefits, and goals achieved. Remaining issues should also be reviewed and closed.
- *Lessons Learned Report* describing risks (threats and opportunistic) and issues (technology, business, organizational, project management) that occurred during the project and the lessons that were learned that can be used to help future projects, cycles.

8.5   Reassign Project Team Members

Toward the end of a project cycle, department managers will start to transition their team members to return to their prior assignments. The PM and the department manager agree on a date when the team member returns to their department. It is the PM's responsibility to ensure project team members complete their tasks and deliverables listed in the Project Schedule and resolve any issues that are open.

8.6   Begin Planning for Next Project Cycle

Before the deployment of the current applications is completed, the PMs for the current and next project cycle can start to plan and hand over resources for the next project cycle.

8.7   Summary

After deploying the current ES, the project team complete the tasks to close the current project cycle. This includes:

- Complete latest changes for computer operations and ES software updates
- Complete other project admin tasks including
  - Close vendor contracts
  - File remaining project documentation
  - Start to run periodic system backup/recovery procedure
- Report project results for this project cycle to the Steering Committee and other stakeholders
- Complete report for lessons learned during this project cycle. Review this report with the PM for the next project cycle
- Obtain signoff from project sponsor that the project work is completed.

The PM for the completed project cycle assists the new PM to prepare the project plan for the next project cycle.

Glossary

Beta Version	A version of software used by a small number of users to identify errors before it is moved to production.
Business Case	A document or presentation that provides the rationale for the organization to acquire, implement, deploy, and support this Enterprise System.
Compliance Test	A test to verify that the software, instruments, or processes used to produce regulated products are compliant with industry and government regulations.
Computer Platform	A computer configuration with the required hardware, operating software, storage, and communication network to accomplish the software development, test, and production of the software.
Configure	Software functionality created using built-in workflow tools shipped by the vendor. To be considered configurable, functionality should be forward-compatible with future releases.
CRM Systems – CustomerRelations Management	System that integrates all functions to plan, market, sell, deliver, and provide customer services, and track sales to customers in specific territories.
Customize	Any functionality that is modified or added to a configured Enterprise System module shipped by the vendor
Data Migration	An activity to help build a new system's data base by making needed changes to records in the legacy system (e.g., correction, adding missing data) and creating programs to transfer the legacy data to the new system.
Deep Dive	An application development method that assists a design team to define a new software application by comparing the OOTB features and functions of the new software to the organization's requirements for the this application.

Deliverable	Something that can be provided during a project (software, document, process, product), as a product or a development process.
Early Adopter	A person who starts to use new technology or product sooner than their peers.
Enterprise System (ES) –	Software product that supports many operations across an enterprise and links data between each system and to a central data base.
ERP Systems Enterprise Resource Planning Systems	Software package that integrates multiple applications for manufacturing, inventory, and other activities. Predecessor to ES
Fit/Gap Analysis	An analysis used to determine which requirements for a planned system fit or have a gap that needs to be fixed.
FRS – Financial Requirement Specification	Specification of requirements for a system that integrates most financial functions for an enterprise.
Functions and Features	Functions describe what something does. Features are the tools that accomplish functions.
Gantt Chart	A bar chart that shows when project tasks should start and end.
HRMS – Human Resource Management System	System that integrates all HR applications for hiring, training, evaluating, assignment, payroll, benefits, personnel data, and other information about each employee.
Out-Of-The-Box (OOTB)	Features and functions of a software product that can be used as part of system immediately after installation without any configuration or customization.
Peer Group Review	Review of project results by an independent team of experts. The purpose is to ensure that the project team has completed their work completely, accurately, and quality standards.
Product Release	Process to deliver a new product to your customer.
Product Road Map	A document that outlines the vision, direction, priorities, and the progress of a product over time
Project	A temporary endeavor undertaken to create a unique result such as a system, service, or product.

Project Management	The tasks to direct a project include planning, organizing. directing, and closing.
Project Implementation Cycle	A method to implement a project by repeating the steps for the first cycle for a series of additional cycles.
Project Implementation Cycle	A method to implement a project by repeating the steps for the first cycle for a series of additional cycles.
RACI Chart	A matrix shows each person's responsibility on a project, which are: R – Responsible to complete task A – Accountable C – Consulted I – Informed
RFP – Request for Proposal	A document that announces a project, details requirements for components, and solicits bids from qualified contractors to complete the project.
SDLC	Standard project management framework used to create software systems. Also called Waterfall Method.
System Administrator	A project role with the responsibility to maintain a list of users of the application and their access to parts of the application, backup, and recovery of programs.
Test Case	A written document that includes the steps to test the functions of a software component.
Test Plan	A list of steps to prepare for and test software to verify its accuracy.
User Group	A group (e.g., department) of individuals who use a system to perform the work for the group.

Bibliography

Davenport, Thomas H., Putting the Enterprise into the Enterprise System, *Harvard Business Review*, 1998, Volume 76, Issue 4, 121–23.

Ries, Peter, *NetSuite for Consultants*, Packt Publishing, 2021.

Thompson, Jeff and Luvai F. Motiwala, *Enterprise Systems For Management, Second Edition*, Prentice Hall, 2012.

Wikipedia, "Enterprise Resource Planning," Wikipedia Foundation, 20,53, 26 September, 2023, https://en.wikipedia.org/wiki/Enterprise_resource_planning

Wikipedia, "Enterprise Software", Wikipedia Foundation, 04:24, 2 August 2023, https://en.wikipedia.org/wiki/Enterprise_software

Index

Note: Page numbers in **bold** refer to tables, and those in *italics* refer to figures.

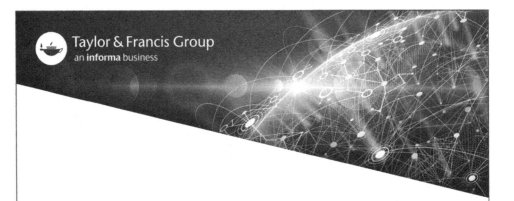

Printed in the United States
by Baker & Taylor Publisher Services